THE
PANDEMIC
PASTOR

Leadership Wisdom for Ministry
During Difficult Times

DR. TAFT QUINCEY HEATLEY

THE
PANDEMIC
PASTOR

CONTENTS

INTRODUCTION

THE Sars-CoV-2 virus has shifted and shaken the world. Our normal is no longer new, and now we are trying to discover how to survive in a pandemic. At the onset of the pandemic, many people did not know what to expect. Some people did not take seriously the warning from scientists that this disease is deadly, and others thought this would pass over and we could continue with life as usual. But we were sadly mistaken.

At the beginning of the pandemic, essential products such as toiletries and disinfectants were being sold at a premium due to high demand and low supply. Cleaning products were flying off the shelves of supermarkets, big box stores, and drugstores, so it was a mad scramble to find an ample supply of disinfectants or hand sanitizer. According to the information we were given from doctors, scientists, and healthcare agencies, we believed that these products would ensure a safe and germ-free environment. But with demand outpacing supply, the cleaning supply industry could not keep up, and many people had to make do or do without. But experiencing a scarcity of certain consumer goods was only one area of our lives that changed dramatically.

The coronavirus pandemic has challenged leaders in every facet of society. This crisis has called into question the policies and practices of corporations and civic organizations. It has exposed the inequities within our nation and within our world, especially in terms of access to health care and support for healthcare professionals. And, of course, the church is not exempt.

The pandemic has shined a light on and in the local church. It has exposed the inadequacies of some ministries and has called into question the relevance of our traditions and religious practices. It has revealed the flaws in the church's systems and structures, as well as exposed the character of its leaders.

Pastors and other church leaders have also come under evaluation. The pandemic has uncovered and unmasked a lack of leadership integrity for some, while illuminating the proper preparedness in others. Additionally, it has given pastors and church leaders opportunities to pivot from an outdated approach to ministry to one that makes sense and is relevant for the current time.

In the early days of the pandemic, pastors employed unique approaches to continue worship and fellowship for church members and to reach out to those persons who were not church members but who needed spiritual support during such a chaotic and confusing time. But all pastors' responses were not the same.

Some pastors refused to believe that COVID-19 was a reality. They believed that the virus was similar to the flu, so they held no regard for the potency of this disease. They sought to ignore it and continued with their regularly scheduled services. Sadly, some pastors lost their lives and endangered the lives of others due to their stubbornness and refusal to adhere to the advice of scientists and other healthcare professionals.

Other religious leaders were cautious but not overly concerned. They monitored the information from the media and sought to keep the congregations they served abreast of any changes. As things progressed, they became more wary of the severity of the virus. They shut down campus worship and closed all activities at their facilities.

However, there was a remnant of pastors who were vigilant and took the virus seriously at the onset. One of my colleagues did so because he and his wife contracted the virus in February 2020. They were stricken with the disease and fought hard for their lives. I am glad to say that they have overcome the virus. For them, it was more than a learning experience. COVID-19 forced them to rethink and reevaluate their approach to ministry.

Interestingly, crisis has a way of doing that. To paraphrase something the Rev. Dr. Martin Luther King Jr. said, you can tell more about what people are made of when they are experiencing adverse conditions as opposed to when they are living in relative calm and comfort.

You may have been a pastor or a leader who was ill-prepared to handle the vicissitudes of ministry during the pandemic. When the mandate went out to limit and close public gatherings, you may have felt that your hands were tied. For you, the church only met if there were people in the physical sanctuary, so you did not know what to do next. You wondered how the ministry would survive financially if members of the congregation were not at church and ceased to give.

Others of you may have invested in a technology infrastructure that included livestreaming and online giving, so it was easier for you to make the transition to online worship. You reasoned that technology was part of your evangelistic efforts to encourage people to stream your service with the hope that eventually they would come to the church building.

Frankly, streaming could have been a means to increase viewership, giving, and membership. But when in-person worship was placed on hold, you had to rely on your streaming platforms as the sole method of worship. You were forced to rethink how you would recreate the sanctuary in the home for you and the people you shepherd.

Perhaps a few of you knew that the digital space was a fertile ground for discipleship. You understood the demographics of your ministry and created a culture that embraced physically distanced discipleship and worship. Given the pandemic, you have searched for ways to increase engagement for believers who may never enter your sanctuary.

Whatever the category in which you discover yourself, I pray that you embrace the truth that hope is available. The pandemic ushered in a time for creativity, spontaneity, and innovation. This is a time for intense devotion to cultivate an environment to hear the voice of the Spirit. This is the time to discern how to be relevant in your presentation of Christ to the world.

Pandemic pastors must be able to discern the times and give attention to the religious symbolism in their churches. We must ask, "Are these symbols necessary, and why?" Pandemic pastors must be flexible and fluid in these times of transition. Keeping your staff, leadership, and congregation engaged is a leadership challenge where over-communication is necessary. Pandemic pastors must have a clear understanding of their congregational culture. This should be analyzed and examined through congregational exegesis.

This book is about the necessity for pastoral leadership during the disruption of the Sars-CoV-2 pandemic on the normalcy of the church. Pandemic pastors—or for that matter, pastors who must shepherd congregations through any type of crisis—must involve the practice of the spiritual disciplines to shape a sensitivity to the Spirit's leading. This should be a normal practice of life for every believer, but particularly pastors.

In this book, you will explore practical tools for worship in the virtual space, the necessity of self-care to maintain your mental health, and the prioritization of family. Essentially, leadership matters, and pandemic pastors must lead with integrity. This attribute is non-negotiable in ministry.

Portions of this book contain excerpts of my final project from my doctor of ministry program at the Candler School of Theology at Emory University. The title of the project is "Pastoral Prophetic Preaching: A Spiritual and Cultural Hermeneutic for Prophetic Speech."

In my estimation, pastors who are preachers participate in the work of exegesis for the preaching moment. Preachers should desire to hear from and be led by the Spirit for prophetic speech. We must understand the makeup of the congregation or audience to whom we preach, but the same work required for proclamation is simultaneously needed for pastoral leadership.

The theory in this approach for preaching is applicable for leading any organization, especially the church. One must practice self-exegesis as well as that of the congregation. Self-exegesis can happen through the practice of the spiritual disciplines.

Congregational exegesis is also vital for leadership. This is the practice of understanding culture: how an organization and a community function, work, and live with one another. The claim is that exegetical work (study of Scripture) for preaching can be applied to leadership. Every pastor—in particular, pandemic pastors—must study, analyze, and constructively critique self and the community in which we serve. This work includes discerning the times.

I reason that the spiritual approach (prayer, study, meditation), coupled with the cultural approach (congregational symbols, traditions, and demographic makeup), are critical to provide relevant and effective leadership at all times. Certainly, this work is necessary for pastoral leadership in crisis.

Pastors and leaders, know yourself (quirks, mental health, what angers and motivates you), the preexisting culture (traditions, history, influencers), and the current culture (expectations of people, emotional health of staff) of the organizations you lead. This methodology to leadership will result in you having a sharper focus as you seek to be a sound and effectual leader. This is the labor and commitment of the pandemic pastor.

At the end of each chapter, there are a set of questions through which leaders can practice self-reflection and self-examination. The reflection can be done in community with a small group or with an accountability partner.

I have found that honest self-reflection and examination is the key to transformation and sanctification. We cannot give a false representation before a holy God who is omniscient. In order to grow personally, especially in our leadership, we must be truthful with ourselves. I pray that you will reflect seriously about your role as a leader of God's people.

CHAPTER ONE

SPIRITUAL PREPAREDNESS: THE OBLIGATION AND DESIRE FOR DEVOTION WITH GOD

"Now in the morning, having risen a long while before daylight, He went out and departed to a solitary place; and there He prayed." (Mark 1:35, NKJV)

JESUS prayed! The Son of God and God the Son prayed. The Second Person of the Holy Trinity prayed. He rose early in the morning to seek direction and guidance from His Father in heaven. Common sense should influence every believer to pray. Frankly, I don't know how we can expect to follow God without speaking to the God who calls us to ministry and leadership. Prayer is essential to know how to lead the church that belongs to Christ! Through prayer, we build intimacy with God and receive direction for leading God's people.

The pastor who engrosses in the spiritual disciplines of prayer, meditation, and devotional reading of Scripture will encounter God's unyielding love for the pastor, the church, and the world. This love for God drives preaching, ministry, and leadership. The Holy Spirit serves as the catalyst to ignite this hunger as the pastor loves God by proclaiming truth. One can only preach the truth of God when one has met the God of love. This love should be the foundational and motivating factor of all ministry activity, especially leadership.

Love is the nature of the YHWH, the God who describes Godself to Moses as recorded in Exodus 34:6-7. This love is shown in the incarnate God, Christ Jesus, the Son of God, who gave His life for the world (John 3:16). Jesus prayed that this love will be with all who believe in Him (John 17:20-26). How befitting that Jesus offered a prophetic prayer that those who would believe the gospel would love God and desire to be one with God! Through the spiritual disciplines, the fire to serve God no matter the circumstance is rekindled as the pastor spends intimate time with God through prayer.

Prayer is the lifeblood of the church and the lifeline for the believer. It is not a coincidence that Jesus took time to steal away and pray to the Father. Prayer as a spiritual discipline is of the utmost necessity for any spiritual leader, and it must be a priority for the church. We need to pray. We must pray. We cannot lead effectively without prayer.

The pandemic has exposed the prayer life of many spiritual leaders, and some of us have discovered where we were and tried to improve and increase our time in prayer. The good news is that God is always available to hear you, but you must be willing to carve out time to meet with God just as Jesus did. Prayer is where you find that you are loved as God leads you in crisis, so prayer is an important spiritual discipline that pastors and spiritual leaders should actively employ.

For pastoral leadership, prayer is essential. The pastor who does not pray does not consider the call to preach, pastor, or lead a worthy one, but only a profession. In private prayer, the Holy Spirit yields power and confidence that God will meet pastors as they serve their congregations.

The nineteenth-century English preacher Charles Haddon Spurgeon regarded prayer as the foremost practice for preachers and pastors. In *Lectures to My Students*, Spurgeon asserts, "All that a college course can do for a student is coarse and external compared with the spiritual and delicate refinement obtained by communion with God."[1]

Spurgeon continues this thought by saying that the understanding of Scripture can only come alive through prayer: "Texts will often refuse to reveal their treasure till you open them with the key of prayer. . . . The closet is the best study. The commentators are good instructors, but the Author Himself is far better, and prayer makes a direct appeal to Him and enlists Him in our cause."[2]

Spurgeon did not speak of prayer as an exercise to support the profession of preaching only. Rather, prayer is essential to the life of the believer and, therefore, the spiritual leader. It is where one discovers the will of God. Jesus as the model example encourages all to pray and the manner in which they should pray (Matthew 6:7-13; Luke 18:1). Our aforementioned Scripture witnesses that Jesus practiced daily prayer (Mark 1:35).

Prayer is crucial for the journey with Christ, and it is the significant means that God uses to transform us where our hearts yearn to know the will and way of God.[3] In prayer, believers can discern the voice of the Spirit calling them to love and to lead God's people. Through prayer, God enlarges the boundaries of the heart as we give ourselves to love God and be loved by God.[4] Prayer centered in love for God will foster a passion for leadership.

It is the spiritual practice of prayer through the years that prepared me to lead our church during this pandemic. Throughout my tenure as pastor, God was calling me to be faithful to Him to make strategic changes in the ministry. It was the aegis of the Holy Spirit that prompted me to increase our presence in the digital space before the pandemic began. This move proved to be beneficial and lifesaving for our church, but it was more than about leadership.

Prayer was the conduit through which I learned to walk with God. Intimacy was the key! It was love for God and, more important, love for the truth that God loved me that created a desire to hear from God. God is my everything! Leadership of God's people should be an outgrowth and an extension of one's desire to please and obey God in every aspect, even when it comes to what is preached to prepare God's people for crisis.

It was the Holy Spirit who instructed me what to preach and from what text to preach in my tenure as pastor. In prayer, God led me to preach certain books for the year. In 2016, the Lord led me to preach through the Book of Exodus. In 2018, God led me to preach through the books of Daniel and Romans. In 2019, God led me to preach through the books of Ezra and Nehemiah. The crux of the matter is that prayer served as the vehicle through which I discerned what to say to God's people and what to do in the time of crisis.

Pastor and leader, if you are going to lead God's people, you must pray and cultivate an environment to hear from God. Prayer is not solely a means to support your profession as preacher. Prayer should be a daily devotional practice for the spiritual leader.

Some pastors viewed the pandemic as an opportunity to reengage God beyond the business and busyness of ministry. Through prayer, a sense of purpose was renewed from a strength gained and given by God. Perhaps this crisis was a call for the church to reconnect with God and to prioritize prayer as an essential practice for the church.

Pastors who focus on prayer for their personal lives and that of their ministries will flourish in a time of crisis, but prayer must move beyond a mere routine and formality for leaders and churches.[5] It must take precedence in the life of the pastor and the church. When this happens, we are in tune with the early church, which held prayer seriously as a response to the directive from Christ.

Every movement of God begins with prayer. (Acts 1:14; 2:42). Yet, prayer is merely one of the spiritual disciplines that cultivates intimacy with God and provides encouragement in crisis. Prayer must accompany an active devotional reading of Scripture.

A steady diet of the word of God presents an opportunity for God to speak. In Scripture, one can find those who seek to love and follow God, even in crisis. God's word is eternal, and it provides instruction for successful navigation in critical waters.

Through engaging Scripture, we discover the love of God and receive the affirmation needed to prevail in life. Through a meditative, devotional reading of Scripture, one seeks a radiant reality of God's love as we meet the God revealed in Scripture.[6] Meditation of God's word, a practice known as *lectio divina*, or holy reading, can draw us closer to God. By using this practice, Christ through the Holy Spirit constructs a sanctuary of the heart, a spiritual and emotional space that serves as a perpetual Eucharist feast in our inner temple.[7]

This kind of meditation is what the twentieth-century mystic Howard Thurman called the "inward journey." Thurman reasoned that through the practice of meditation, one can experience the gift considered to be the purest form of love: the love of God in Christ Jesus.[8]

In meditation and meditative reading, God increases our imagination to be used for God's good purposes. This living with God is the Christian idea of incarnation where God uses our imagination to teach us about the world God desires.[9] Maintaining a devotional reading of Scripture was critical for me in quarantine and in the pandemic.

At the onset of the pandemic, I was inspired to read one chapter of Proverbs and five psalms daily. I continued this practice for months until I felt the unction of the Holy Spirit to read each of the Gospels during the Lenten season. I invited the church to join me in this devotional quest, and my hope was that the congregation would nurture deeper intimacy with God.

We continued this practice throughout the year. It has proven to accelerate the spiritual maturity of the congregation. Furthermore, it connected pastor and people by building trust between the two as we both seek God together. Yet, there is more that I found. A meditative reading of Scripture should be mirrored with the discipline of studying Scripture.

The pastor as leader is one who actively studies Scripture. Akin to meditative reading, the discipline of studying Scripture, too, is incarnational. In this practice, one seeks to experience God to be changed as one interprets what is read.[10] Interpretation is foremost before application. Through this discipline of study, the pastor ascertains the life transforming truth that revolutionizes life as the Spirit reveals the meaning of the author written into a particular community.

It is the study of Scripture that furnishes an empirical framework in which meditation functions successfully.[11] Through the study of Scripture, the pastor experiences the love of God and witnesses this love through those who lived in community with God through many generations.

The study of Scripture should be a disciplinary practice of pastoral leaders. They must not only be well-versed in Scripture to discern the will of God, but also should seek to meet God in Scripture through the Holy Spirit. The Bible must not be viewed as a tool, but as the conduit through which pastors experience God. Pastors should be what Brent Strawn labels as the "scribe-king" of Deuteronomy 17.

Pastors who are leaders in their communities facilitate community engagement with God's word in order to serve as those who know the law of God.[12] Those who know the law simultaneously know to follow it. This deep encounter with God's word facilitates a love of God's word. Then other spiritual disciplines, such as fasting, help unclog the lines of communication from God's mouth to our hearts. Ultimately, God is to be sought after first with all of our heart (Jeremiah 29:13).

Carving out time with God is not easy; and if you are like me, then you understand just how challenging it is to pray consistently. Life and its responsibilities compete for our time, which can seem to be elusive each day. Honestly, it was a struggle for me to maintain a consistent time to meet with God at the onset of the pandemic. I prayed each day and did so multiple times, but the pandemic forced me to change my intimate devotional time with God. I discovered that the best time for me to practice the spiritual disciplines was in the early morning hours before my family arose.

When I was an unmarried minister with no children, it was easier for me to pray and to spend time with God in the evening. But marriage and parenthood have a way of disrupting normal routines. Because of virtual school, my wife and I had to shift our schedules and be present for our children. Normally, I would pray at 9:00 AM, study Scripture at 10:00 AM, and then attack my to-do list for the day; but the pandemic interrupted all of this.

Instead of praying and reading Scripture during the mid-morning hours, I served as the in-home teacher's assistant for my son's kindergarten class between the hours of 9:00 and 11:00 AM, Monday through Friday. It was a struggle to keep a five-year-old engaged in virtual learning, especially because I was not trained for that type of work. Yet, I could not forsake my responsibility as a parent, nor could I forget that I needed to spend precious time with God. Therefore, I had to make a shift and become an early-morning person.

This meant waking up earlier than I was accustomed to doing. This is a challenge for anyone, like me, who deems sleep to be a therapeutic pastime. I would rise between 4:00 AM and 5:00 AM to pray and read and study Scripture. It was and continues to be invaluable to hear God speak and give direction for my life, family, and the congregation where I serve. Prayerfully, you also discovered God anew during the time of quarantine as you actively communicated with God and built intimacy.

Pastors, as you employ the spiritual disciplines as necessary activities for your life, you will discover how God will prepare you for crisis and difficult times. Just know that you must humbly position yourself before God, seeking to hear and to obey what God desires for you and the ministry where you have been called.

A grateful and submissive attitude is the correct posture of prayer for pastoral leaders. It is through a consistent devotion to God that pastors and leaders ascertain more clearly and meekly acknowledge that they do not own the church (the people) they serve. The church belongs to

Christ. The pandemic has highlighted this truth, and it is this notion to which we turn next.

Leader Examination

- Be honest. How often do you pray to hear from God? How often do you study Scripture to seek God?

- Are your prayers a means to support preaching only? Is your study of Scripture a means to support preaching only?

- Is prayer a practice for your leadership daily, or do you use it more for times of crises?

- Is there a set time for devotional engagement of the spiritual disciplines? If so, how do you protect this time?

- When is the best time of the day when you have uninterrupted quietness? Your devotional time with God should happen there.

Prayer for Pandemic Pastors and Leaders:

Lord God, I desire to walk closely with You. I yield to Your sovereignty and power in my life. Help me to create a place of intimacy in prayer with You so that I may hear You speaking to me. Wake me to rise early to pray. Speak to me in the midnight hour when I am at rest. Alert me when

I should call on Your name. Create in me a hunger for Your word where I discern that You meet me in Your word in my time of reading.

I desire to discover Your leadership of my life as I seek to give leadership for what You have given me stewardship over. I am Yours, and I desire to be led by You. Please, Lord, lead me so that I can lead Your people with integrity and truth. In the name of Jesus, I pray. Amen.

[1]Charles H. Spurgeon, *Lectures to My Students* (Grand Rapids, MI: Zondervan, 1954), 43.
[2]Ibid.
[3]Richard J. Foster, *The Celebration of Discipline*, Third Edition (New York: Harper One, 1998), 33-37.
[4]Howard Thurman, *Meditations of the Heart* (Boston: Beacon Press, 1981), 47-49.
[5]Thom S. Rainer, *The Post-Quarantine Church* (Carol Stream, IL: Tyndale Momentum, 2020), 57.
[6]Richard J. Foster, *The Celebration of Discipline*, 19.
[7]Ibid, 20.
[8]Howard Thurman, *For the Inward Journey* (Richmond, Indiana: Friends United Press, 1961), 91-92.
[9]Richard J. Foster, *The Celebration of Discipline*, 26.
[10]Ibid, 69.
[11]Ibid, 64.
[12]Brent A. Strawn, *The Old Testament Is Dying: A Diagnosis and Recommended Treatment* (Baker Academic, 2017), 200.

CHAPTER TWO

THE CHURCH BELONGS TO CHRIST: THE DANGER OF PRIDE AND RELIGIOUS SYMBOLISM

"But who do you say that I am? Simon Peter answered and said, 'You are the Christ, the Son of the living God.' Jesus answered and said to him, 'Blessed are you, Simon Bar-Jonah, for flesh and blood has not revealed this to you, but My Father who is in heaven. And I also say to you that you are Peter, and on this rock I will build My church, and the gates of Hades shall not prevail against it.'" (Matthew 16:15-18, NKJV)

IN Matthew 16:15-18, Jesus asks a pertinent question to the disciples. By this time, Jesus' fame had continued to expand. Jesus of Nazareth was known in Galilee, and His teaching, miracles, signs, and wonders had captivated many but repulsed others. The people of ancient Israel and Palestine had thoughts concerning this prophet from Nazareth, and it prompted Jesus to ask His disciples about His identity.

Jesus asked the disciples who the people said He was. They responded that He was a prophet or the second coming of Elijah or Jeremiah. But Jesus got personal and asked a penetrating question to those who were supposed to know Him. He wanted to hear what the disciples thought. Who was He to *them*? They had left everything to follow Him, and they had been front and center at the miraculous display of power. Who did *they* say He was?

In that moment, only the bold and impetuous Simon dared to answer the question, and his reply is priceless: "You are the Messiah, the Son of the living God."

Jesus revealed to Simon that God in heaven had revealed this truth to him. Then Jesus commissioned Simon and gave him a new identity that would cement his place in history. Jesus called him "Peter," which means "rock."

Jesus then gave a prophetic word of power and victory over the supernatural forces of evil. The church will not succumb to the powers of hell. Yet, it is the declarative statement of ownership that is equally compelling. Jesus said, "On this rock I will build *my* church" (emphasis added). By this statement, Jesus was commissioning His leader as well as claiming responsibility and ownership of the church: The church belongs to Christ.

The church is the body of Christ. No denominational identity, tradition, or orthodoxy can subvert the truth that the Christian church belongs to Christ. It bears His name because Christ bore the marks for His body. The church shares His name because He shed His blood for His body.

Jesus gave His life for His church (1 John 3:16), and He is the sole proprietor of the church.

Pastors and ministry leaders are merely managers of Jesus' property—His people whom He bought at a price (1 Corinthians 6:20). No pastor, bishop, elder, diocese, council, session, or joint board has ownership of His church. These groups are comprised of believers who carry a responsibility to effectively administer and live out what Jesus has spoken. In the church of the living God, Jesus is King.

The church is a theocracy, meaning that it is not a democratic state where votes have the authority. For many people, this is difficult to accept because we live in a country that prizes democracy. This is not to suggest that members, committees, and teams do not have a voice or that their thoughts, feelings, and opinions are irrelevant.

However, the church's theocratic nature refers to the one who holds ultimate authority in the church. What the Lord says reigns, and He is the authority of His church. Every church leader should submit to the wisdom of Christ by the power of the Holy Spirit to carry out Christ's desires as spoken through generations by the word of God.

Before any plan, strategy, or action is formed, Christ should and must be consulted because it is His church, and only He knows what His church needs in every moment of existence. The tragedy of leadership in the church is when pastors act as kings or queens of their congregations for which they have never given their lives.

Only one has had His flesh nailed to a tree in a gruesome display of capital punishment for the lives of all who choose to believe. Only Christ gave His life for His body, so our hope rests in Him. Therefore, His church should pay homage to its only head (Colossians 1:18) by meditating on His word and praying to seek guidance for how to lead His people.

This is not an easy task, but it is one that requires humility and patience. Sadly, many pastors have fallen victim to the success of thinking that the church is their responsibility and cannot function without them. Some pastors feel that the "show" of ministry is not successful unless they are at the center of all things church. Pulpits are now stages, where their performance or act is before the people. The role of their team or subordinates is to make the pastor look good as opposed to exalting Christ.

Some pastors feel that they are the "draw" that fills their sanctuaries. That is, they believe that it is their voice that beckons people to place their trust in Christ and come to church each week. This is a dangerous mindset for pastors to have because it leads to the sin of pride. These pastors fail to realize that but by the grace of God they have life and are able to speak about God's saving grace. However, as I have had to learn to navigate through this chaotic time, I have discovered that the pandemic is challenging this prideful notion of many pastors and has illuminated this hazard to spiritual maturity.

Danger of Pride

"When pride comes, then comes shame; but with the humble is wisdom" (Proverbs 11:2, NKJV). The word *pride* has various meanings, but the word usually describes how a person can be centered upon self. The Hebrew word translated "pride," *zādôn,* means "overconfidence" or "presumptuousness." It refers to an unreasonable and inordinate self-esteem or self-entitlement.

People who are proud presume too much in their favor, especially in the sense of authority.[1] They believe that authority rests with them and they have absolute autonomy in the affairs pertaining to God. But prideful people—in particular, pastors—must recognize that they, too, are people under authority. Failure to do this results in the sin of rebellion or disobedience, which is a variation of pride, according to the understanding of the word from Scripture (1 Samuel 15:23).

People who are proud assert their own will to the point of rebelling against one in authority over them.[2] The dangers of pride are illuminated in the story of Saul and his struggle to follow God.

Saul, the Benjamite from Kish, was chosen to be Israel's king, but he was presumptuous and rebellious toward Yahweh. On two occasions, he failed to adhere to the instruction from YHWH through the prophet, priest, and judge Samuel. In 1 Samuel 13, Saul acts rashly. He offered a sacrifice to inquire of the Lord. The offering of sacrifices was the role of the priest, not the king, but Saul was impatient and felt compelled to offer a sacrifice to inquire whether to go to war (1 Samuel 13:12).

In his haste, Saul disobeyed Samuel's command. This act of disobedience began a strand of terrible decisions that would lead to the loss of his kingship. As recorded in 1 Samuel 15, Saul disobeyed God by taking spoil from the battle when he was instructed not to. He felt that the spoil could be used to offer sacrifices to God for what YHWH had allowed Israel to achieve. However, Saul was disobedient, thinking that he knew better than God.

In his rebuke of Saul, Samuel offered the following words of Scripture: "Does the LORD delight in burnt offerings and sacrifices as much as in obeying the LORD? To obey is better than sacrifice, and to heed is better than the fat of rams" (1 Samuel 15:22, NIV).

Saul fell victim to the pride of early success and self-entitlement. He believed that because he was king of Israel, the world revolved around him and that he was not subject to the authority of God. Ultimately, it cost him the throne of Israel and brought shame to his legacy. Every religious leader should consider the errors of pride and how hazardous it could be to one's legacy.

The role of pastor and spiritual leader is dangerous because it is easy to fall into the trap of celebrity and fame in any congregation. Every Sunday, the pastor stands before the people to give words from the living word. Your message penetrates the hearts and minds of those searching for truth. People are vulnerable and hurt, and they are looking to hear from the God in you, especially in times of crisis. When you speak with the power of God, they will laud you and heap praise upon your name. They will present you with gifts and grant honor and respect to your name.

That type of confirmation can be consuming. You may yearn for the applause of amens, head nods, and agreement as you break the bread of life; but you must remember that you are a servant under authority who serves bread that you did not buy or bake. Jesus Christ is the bread of life (John 6:35), not you. You were not put in the oven! You did not have to endure the temperature of the sun against your broken and battered body! You did not die for this bread, but it was freely given to you to eat and to share (Matthew 26:26).

With that in mind, your words should be crafted carefully with precision to honor and magnify the one who called you to rightfully divide the word of truth. But you must remember that you are not the one to whom they look. If people are looking to you as the savior, you are flirting with idolatry, which is antithetical to the will of Yahweh (Exodus 20:2-5).

It is a struggle, but pastors, preachers, and leaders must not succumb to the place where the ministry they serve consoles their insecurity to be accepted. We are all human, and we all have a need to be uplifted and affirmed, but the pulpit is not the place for this kind of affirmation. Instead, we should seek that in the private devotional space with Christ, the owner of the church.

In prayer and meditation with God is where you find the support and encouragement for your life, call, and work. The support for your ministry cannot and should not be measured by your Sunday morning performance because any gathering of the people of God is not about you. The church is and shall forever be about Christ, and this truth has been amplified during the coronavirus pandemic.

COVID-19 has forced pastors and leaders to evaluate and critique methodologies and ideologies in ministry. When it became a health hazard to physically meet in the sanctuary to worship God, it caused many of us to question our orthopraxy and what we should prioritize. Is Christ sending a message to His church in the pandemic? If the church belongs to Christ, then what is Christ saying about and to His church at this moment in history?

In Galatians 1:10, the apostle Paul poses a question to the church that is deceived. The Galatian church questioned the validity of the gospel of grace that Paul had preached to them. His question is profound because it serves as a measuring rod, a litmus test, for any pastor, preacher, minister, or servant of God: "Am I now trying to win the approval of human beings, or of God? Or am I trying to please people? If I were still trying to please people, I would not be a servant of Christ" (NIV).

The question raises the issue: What is the gospel directed to, and to whom shall it be pleasing? If this question did not resonate before the pandemic, it surely should boom loudly now. The pandemic has shifted life as we know it. It has caused us to question daily practices that were once normal but now could be detrimental to one's health. Something as simple as gathering in close proximity could result in transmission of a disease that could lead to death. This calls into question our worship culture, traditions, and practices that we hold to be sacred.

I must admit, it has been challenging to preach to an empty sanctuary. Preaching is a central element of our worship, and the custom of an audible call and response is typical in many congregations within my context. Preaching to a camera inside an empty sanctuary gives new meaning to the term "Can I get a witness?" Your witnesses may be there, but you cannot hear them respond.

You can't rely on the responses of "Amen!" "I hear you, preacher!" "Well!" or even hand clapping, a head nod, or the lifting of hands. The encouragement in the preaching moment must come from within. Preachers must bring amens with them, which should be standard practice at any time. For some, preaching during the pandemic has been an ego-disrupter.

Many people consider the gift of speech and the rhetorical style, alongside the musicality of the preacher, to be necessary to inspire, motivate, and move the crowd. (This is preaching in my cultural context and tradition, the African American or black church.) Some preachers feed off of the engagement with the congregation as a sign of affirmation and encouragement. Many preachers are accustomed to a congregation with listeners who hope to feel the combination of style and substance from the message.

In this context, preaching is not only heard, but also it is felt and shared in community. James Harris describes the preaching moment as a relational experience he expresses as a "We–Thou" encounter of the black church.[3] In the black church tradition, the We–Thou relationship involves three parties: the preacher, the congregation, and the power of the Holy Spirit.[4]

Preaching on Sunday morning is a true communal instance. For Harris, "the sermon is really a congregational activity, a dialogue where a host of persons get involved in the preaching and hearing process."[5] It is a communal experience that is a participatory theological exercise.

To help in this process, the organist is ready to find the key of the preacher's voice as he or she is ready to close the sermon (the celebratory climax). The melodic presentation of voice inflections by the preacher helps move the sermon and the congregation. It can be pleasing to the ear and the heart. This practice is wonderful when all parties are able to participate, but the COVID church has challenged these notions and, in turn, may have damaged the ego.

In quarantine worship, we were forced to ask, Are all our practices necessary given the climate of the new normal? Should we follow tradition for the sake of familiarity? Am I dependent on the help of the music and the approval of the congregation? Is my sermon judged by the response of the people? If so, what will I do when the people are no longer here? Paul's question in Galatians becomes relevant: "Are we seeking to please humans or the Lord?"

Preachers—in particular, black preachers—are not disc jockeys. We do not spin the tunes of words to illicit movement and unity for the sake of entertainment. The core of the preaching task is to proclaim the good news of Christ, even in times when it may not feel good. Our primary goal is never to please the itching ears of those who listen. Rather, it is to magnify and glorify our Lord as we faithfully declare that Jesus is Lord. Human approval should not be a priority. Even if it is desired, it must be placed in its proper perspective.

We minister before an audience of one, to whom the congregation belongs. The accompaniment of musicians present in the preaching moment may not be necessary, even if it is customary, especially if coming to the sanctuary endangers the lives of those you are called to shepherd. Quarantine worship compelled me to think as a shepherd more so than that of a preacher.

In one staff meeting about six months into quarantine worship, the minister of music informed me that the music director and percussionist were ready to come into the sanctuary and assist me in the worship service (that is, back me up in the preaching moment). All I needed to do was give them the word, and they would be there. I posed the question to the staff. Some of them thought it would enhance the virtual worship experience, and others were indifferent.

While the musicians would be socially distanced and away from me, I did not yet sense the Holy Spirit urging me to pursue this inquiry. For me, the heart of the issue was the safety of our employees and members. Some people on our ministry team have yet to be vaccinated, so it did not sit well with me that there was the potential of exposing the virus to one another, which could result in harm to the entire congregation. I made a decision to keep our musical presentations virtual and depend on the Lord for my help when preaching.

I do not wish to cast aspersions on pastors who have people in the congregation with them when they preach, whether it be the worship team or members of the congregation who are appropriately socially distanced. The beauty of the kingdom and culture is that we have the liberty to do what we feel is suitable for the culture and communities we serve. The question is about our motivation. What is the "why"?

I felt that given my context and culture, safety was, and still is, the priority. If it means I preach to myself, by myself, so be it. But in reality, I never preach to an empty room. Heaven is listening and watching. The audience of one is ever present because our God is the omnipresent God! Worship in the pandemic has taught me to be more authentic in our worship presentations. No matter the tradition, culture, or style of worship, authenticity is a priority.

The church where I serve as pastor has sought a culture of genuine worship. Our first worship service in the COVID era was the 157th church anniversary service in March 2020. Our worship team included a praise team ensemble of six, a worship leader, a four-person band, a two-person media team, and me. We thought that we could maintain this group throughout the pandemic, but we soon realized that in doing so we were putting people in danger. The infection rates were increasing, and the transmission of the virus was out of control.

After a conversation with the minister of music, we began to explore a number of ways that we could create a safe worship environment that did not place our members and worship teams at risk. This move impelled us to rely more on the technology we already owned. Given the reality of the pandemic, I wonder if God is exposing unnecessary practices to which many people have asserted a measure of divinity? Is the crisis a revelation of what is essential for worship?

Scripture is clear. The church is the body of Christ (1 Corinthians 12). Since Christ gave His life for His body, it is crucial that He be the focal point of ministry. Everything that the church is and everything that the church does should have Christ at the center, and He is the reason we gather. It is in Him that we live, move, and have our being (Acts 17:28).

Christ becomes the goal of our existence. Thus, as we present Christ to the world, we must ask, Do our symbols promote Christ as the center of our message? Our symbols matter, especially in this COVID era of church.

Religious Symbols Matter

The coronavirus pandemic has cast a light on our religious practices, exposed how we do ministry, and forced us to look honestly at the ways we worship. The advent of the COVID era exposed this epidemic of being ill-prepared in the church. Simply stated, many churches were not ready to transition in this digital age. Leaders were unable or unwilling to make the shift. These leaders held fast to their traditions and praxis and refused to discern the times. They held fast to the symbols of their respective traditions and failed to ask the critical questions as to what matters and why.

This perspective is understandable, especially if the people in the congregation refuse to move with the times. But if the church wants to be relevant to this age, it must transition into it and not lose the central message of the gospel: Jesus saves. Certainly, this is possible. One of the ways the church can be relevant and maintain its focus is through its symbolism.

Every church has its symbols to which it attributes significance. Just look around. If you were to look in the sanctuary, you would see multiple symbols, especially in churches that place a high premium on tradition. The symbols range from pews, stained-glass windows, plaques, and pictures, just to name a few. Such is the case for the church where I pastor.

In our worship center, the pews have name placards on them that people hold dear. Some members will only sit on the pew their family donated and would not welcome others to sit in that space unless the family approved. But there is one symbol that many people feel solidifies its identity: the historic sanctuary of Shiloh Baptist Church.

The historic sanctuary is located at 1401 Duke Street. The cornerstone was laid in 1891, and the building was completed in 1893. For most of Shiloh's history, the historic sanctuary was the place of worship. Most of the congregation came to know Christ in that building, which holds such significance as a religious symbol that a small replica of the building is part of the church's logo.

The historic sanctuary has significance, but it is not the place where we currently worship. Since 2005, Shiloh has held its services in the worship center located at 1401 Jamieson Avenue. Although the historic sanctuary is used quite frequently, it is not the main place of worship, but its symbolism is prevalent. The question of this symbolism, which is part of our tradition, came into question during the pandemic.

In the quarantine church, there is no building in which we worship, and the pandemic illuminated this important factor of our ministry during this time. We realized that the majority of our logo is comprised of a representation of our historic sanctuary, a building that speaks to our history but remains empty on Sunday mornings. This is the symbol we were giving to the world.

However, if no one could enter our current sanctuary due to quarantine, let alone the historic sanctuary we have not used for worship in quite some time, why would we promote the building through the logo? After we moved our Sunday services to the worship center in 2005, we created the logo to preserve the memory of the historic sanctuary. So, by 2021, we had been using this logo for about 16 years. But when I looked more intently at our messages from the digital space, it became apparent that our logo had to change.

SHILOH
BAPTIST CHURCH
—— EST. 1863 ——

The sentiment behind the creation of the historic sanctuary logo pointed to the faithfulness of God, who gave strength to our ancestors who had helped construct the original building. The gesture was noble and noteworthy. But when the pandemic hit, we had to raise the question of relevancy: If our logo promotes a building that we do not worship in regularly during a time when we do not even worship in brick-and-mortar buildings, what communication are we sending to the world? The logo does highlight the cross, but the building still takes center stage.

I believed that this was inconsistent messaging to the world about who we are and what we promote. So, we developed a new logo to speak to the world and to communicate what is central to our being. That message is that we are the church of the living God redeemed by Jesus Christ. The symbol that conveys this truth is the cross, not the building.

The story of our ministry, tradition, and belief culminates with the cross of Calvary. It is the moment of human history that joins the church together. We are not the church except by Jesus Christ, who gave His life on the cross, and that cross is now in the center of our worship space. The cross is a symbol at our Communion table as well as the largest symbol in our worship center. If there is one symbol to which we give to the world about our confession of faith, it should be the cross.

The historic sanctuary in our logo would be functional if we were worshiping in the building, but we decided to change our logo to be consistent about our current messaging. Many churches have logos in which their building is the focus, and this serves as a point of reference for people to see where they worship. But this is not the case for Shiloh anymore.

Since the church is the people and not the building, it was important to centralize the reason why we gather, albeit virtually. Because we held no in-person worship services, it was not paramount to promote a place where people could not enter or have a frame of reference. We wanted people to know that when they see Shiloh, they can see the cross. Christ is what matters the most at our church, so we made the cross the main symbol of our logo to remember to keep Christ as the focus of everything we do.

The theology of the new design is the centralization of the cross. The cross now represents the letter *I* in *Shiloh*. Christ is central to who we are as the church, and He is the sole reason we are the church. The *I* that is the cross represents Christ's unselfishness when He laid down His life and then called us to deny ourselves and take up our cross and follow Him (Luke 9:23).

Furthermore, the *I* is related to the first-person pronoun that is part of the first-person singular of the verb *be*, which is *I am*. Etymologically, *I am* in the Greek of the New Testament is translated "ego." Christ is the "I am"! Therefore, the taking up of our cross is the laying down of our egos as we worship the Great "I am."

The new logo represents a shift into a new normal. The virtual church has created home sanctuaries. When people come to church, they do so from their homes. The message that we promote through our image is about the one who remains the unifying agent of our faith.

We gather in the name of Jesus, and He is the one who transitions the emblem of the cross from one of suffering, shame, and rebellion into one of liberation, life, and love. It is because of His act of love on the cross that we gather to give honor and reverence to Him. Every other symbol of our faith is ancillary to that of the cross, which highlights the truth that the church belongs to Christ.

Worship in the pandemic illuminated the intentionality of our messaging and images. Furthermore, it forced us to shift through our processes and how we operate as a ministry. Through our analysis, we were compelled to embrace the truth that virtual ministry would become a staple for us. It would be important for us to focus our attention and shift resources to its improvement for the future.

Leader Examination

- Where did you preach each Sunday during quarantine worship? How challenging has it been to preach to an empty sanctuary? Did you feel that you were part of a community preaching to a computer screen or a camera?

- As a pastor, do you wrestle with pride? Do you feel that the pulpit has come to be more about you and your agenda as opposed to that of Christ? How?

- In what ways do you work to maintain humility in your approach to ministry? Has pastoring in the pandemic helped or hindered?

- How reliant were you on people being physically present to preach and pastor?

- What messages do the symbols in your ministry or organization send? Are there symbols (or people) in your ministry that could be considered as religious idols?

- Is there a meaning or theology behind your logo and ministry symbols?

Prayer for Pandemic Pastors and Leaders:

My Lord and my God, I have a desire to do Your will. Please reveal to me the places where I have not acknowledged You and where I have thought too highly of myself, not recognizing that I am because You are.

I humbly submit my work as my worship unto You. Remove every ounce of self-pride in me, and convict me when pride seeks to consume. I am Yours, Lord. You are the head of the church, and it belongs to You.

Forgive me for my prideful approach to serve You. Create in me a clean and humble heart before You. Please put this truth ever before me. I join with Your servant David and cry, "Search me, O God, and know my heart; Try me, and know my anxieties; And see if there is any wicked way in me, And lead me in the way everlasting" (Psalm 139:23-24, NKJV).

Reveal to me any traditions or symbols in your church that do not glorify You nor are pleasing in Your sight. Reveal to me what I need to remove or restore in Your church. Grant me the courage to stand for You so that You are highly exalted in Your church. You are my end-all and be-all. My desire is to worship, glorify, and please You in my leadership of Your people. This I ask in the name of Jesus. Amen.

---

[1] R. L. Harris, G. L. Archer Jr., and B. K. Waltke (Eds.), *Theological Wordbook of the Old Testament* (Chicago: Moody Press, 1999), electronic ed., 239.
[2] Ibid.
[3] Author James Harris contends the "We-Thou" moment differs from the "I-Thou" relationship that Martin Buber notes in preaching. See more of the issue of the nexus between style and substance of the sermon in *Preaching Liberation*.
[4] James Harris, *Preaching Liberation* (Minneapolis: Fortress Press, 1995), 64.
[5] Ibid, 65.

CHAPTER THREE

THE DISCOVERY AND NECESSITY FOR VIRTUAL MINISTRY

"To the Jews I became like as a Jew, that I might win Jews; to those who are under the law, as under the law, that I might win those who are under the law; to those who are without law, as without law (not being without law toward God, but under law toward Christ), that I might win those who are without law; to the weak I became as weak, that I might win the weak. I have become all things to all men, that I might by all means save some. Now this I do for the gospel's sake, that I may be partaker of it with you." (1 Corinthians 9:20-23, NKJV)

O UR first Sunday in the COVID/quarantine church was Sunday, March 22, 2020. Due to our concern for the health and safety of the church, only the worship personnel (audiovisual technician, praise team, musicians), totaling 12 people, accompanied me into our worship center. The service was succinct and short, so we were surprised by the volume of engagement on our streaming platform (over 3,500 people viewed the service). By chance, we felt that we had discovered the formula for quarantine worship, but this was only the beginning. We knew we had to shift and decide how we were going to be the church at the onset and during this crisis. We recognized that we would have to transition to a virtual church.

Crises in life are inevitable. Bad things do happen to good people. This truth has been magnified during the coronavirus pandemic. Families are grieving loved ones who have succumbed to the deadly grip of the virus. Others are stressed because they are no longer employed. Children are being homeschooled, and parents are getting a crash course on the duality of being an educator and a working professional.

There are a host of other challenges that we have had to address, and we grapple to adapt to the new normal in our society and culture. Certainly, this has affected the church and the way we present ministry.

Once the coronavirus became a pandemic, ministry became a challenge. No longer could congregations gather in mass numbers. Our customary approach to the worship service had to be revised, and ministries responded in different ways. Some churches sought to continue gathering in person, albeit in small numbers, while others ignored the guidance of the Centers for Disease Control and Prevention (CDC) and continued to meet each week. Many of these churches exposed their congregants to the virus, and subsequently many of those congregants died.

Other churches heeded the warning and followed the ordinances of their states' health department. They did not meet physically but held service and prayer meeting via teleconference. There are many churches who continue to meet virtually each week. Because of their preparation and online presence, they have thrived during the pandemic.

The virtual church, or church online, is not a new phenomenon. Since the turn of the twenty-first century, many megachurches that possessed the resources to have a television presence consequently livestreamed their services. Initially, the livestream was used to help members who could not worship in person, including those who were sick or homebound, those who worked on Sunday, and even members who were on vacation but still wanted to worship while they were away.

However, the online church brought with it another factor. Whether by happenstance or strategy, churches that invested in online ministry recognized it as another means of evangelism. The online church expanded the reach of ministry, and now services via websites viewed on smartphones or tablets meant that people could attend church from multiple locations. Ministries could reach different continents and bring the gospel to different places, while simultaneously worshiping physically at one location.

This new virtual church augmented ministry, and those who welcomed it saw opportunity for growth. Some churches even have designated staff and volunteers exclusively for the online church. I know of ministries who have online associate pastors to connect with online worshipers.

Still, many church leaders and members viewed the online church as members being apathetic and lazy. It brought a negative connotation for those who chose to worship at home but not come to the building. Some pastors and church staff thought dedicating resources to technology was unnecessary and wasteful. This happened to be the case for me in my ministry context.

When I became a senior pastor, one of my first objectives was to increase the online presence at the ministry I served. I viewed this to be instrumental to the future growth of the ministry. I am a Generation Xer, and I was 40 when I became pastor. I reasoned that a relevant online presence was necessary to thrive in ministry.

Upon arrival at Shiloh, I encouraged us to hire a communications and marketing director to help synchronize our messages to the public. A large part of that responsibility was finding a reputable streaming provider for our service, as well as enhancing our online giving platform. We found a streaming host and a new giving platform within the first year of my pastorate in 2016. I surmised that these improvements would help our visibility as a ministry and increase our evangelistic efforts. It happened, but the costs associated with this transition were met with resistance.

Some people within our leadership could not see the need to invest in a technology infrastructure. They saw

The Pandemic Pastor

streaming as a luxury and not a necessity. They viewed it to be an expensive venture. They frowned upon members who would not come to the sanctuary for worship, and they asked, "Why can't people just get up on Sunday and come to church?" "Won't our membership decrease if people do not come to church?" "Why pay processing fees for people to give online?" "Why can't they just write a check like the rest of us?" "Why must people be on their phones all the time?"

Ultimately, many church leaders reasoned that the virtual church would hurt and hinder the physical church. They believed that an online presence would create a culture of indifference to attending church. They could not envision people being introduced to a ministry via a smartphone or a tablet. For them, the only way to meet Christ was to cross the threshold of the church building and gather physically with people in the sanctuary.

Honestly, there is a measure of truth to their sentiments. It is good for people to gather in community to exalt Christ. No good Christian would debate that. But while I welcomed their opinions, I tried to help them understand that we were ignoring a huge segment of the community to whom I felt that God was calling us. Unfortunately, these church leaders failed to realize that we were trying to do ministry in a post-Christian society using methods from a prior age.

A post-Christian society is one where the superiority of a Christian worldview has subsided. The indication of this truth is the fact that there has been a drastic decline in the number of people who participate in religious activity and practices, such as study of Scripture, prayer, and church attendance.[1] According to the Pew Research Center, in the last ten years, America has witnessed a 12-percent decline of those who identify as Christian.[2] This decline has been happening for a while, in particular at the turn of the century.

In the research performed by the Barna Group, it was noted that the unchurched demographic, those who have never attended church services or are currently on a hiatus from the church, continues to rise in America, representing 43 percent of the population.[3] Moreover, much of this is contributed to the unattractive nature of churches that have a negative view of technology and its use in church.

For the unchurched, the church is not in touch with reality. Therefore, to be attractive in a post-Christian society, the faith community must invest in and channel their digital resources to engage the world and to connect with the world where it is.[4] The world has become digitized, so it behooves the church to do likewise with our methods. One of those ways is rethinking how people worship financially.

Many in the church could not fathom people giving online. Simply because they had always given by writing checks and giving cash, they assumed it would be easier for everyone to give in this same cookie-cutter way. I spent a lot of time explaining that this is a generational issue.

For example, I rarely write checks. I pay all of my bills via online banking, and most of the people in my generation do the same. They transfer money to one another via CashApp, Venmo, or Zelle.

The finance team at my church simply could not envision this. To them it was an unnecessary waste. Eventually, they did yield to my leading, but they did so reluctantly. They did not withhold their opinions regarding the matter, but given the future of our church and its ministry, I had to be stern.

Irrespective of the church culture I inherited, I knew that the times were too critical for us. We were stunting growth and quickly becoming irrelevant because our approach to ministry was out of touch, if not already outdated. The people we were hoping to attract lived and worked with technology, so it was critical for us to continue to become a ministry whose methods, processes, and presentations were integrated into the lives and priorities of the generations who had left the church but still loved Christ—hence, relevant.[5] I knew that if we weren't careful, we would rapidly become an out-of-touch ministry.

But to their credit, the members of the finance team were not illogical. They spoke from their existential reality. Their points were valid, but their overall perspective was limited. It was simply a matter of the generational divide where some could not see the importance of a virtual ministry.

Most of the leadership in ministry are Builders (born before 1946) and Boomers (born 1946-1964), and they were all reared in church. I am a Generation Xer (the generation born between 1965-1981), and my wife is a Millennial (the generation born between 1982-1999). We are raising two Generation Z children (born 2000 and beyond). The Boomers in our church could never imagine worshiping via church online—many did not even have a smartphone—but our current world is heavily influenced by technology.

Computers, phones, and laptops are the norm in mostly every industry, especially in education, medicine, and business. Business meetings and distance learning are conducted via Zoom, GoTo Meetings, Adobe Connect, WebEx, and Microsoft Teams. With the advent of PayPal, Venmo, Zelle, and the Square, and improvements in online banking, most financial transactions are handled electronically.

The entire world functions through technology. So, if technology is a huge part of normative society and culture, the church cannot be ignorant to think that it can be relevant and thrive without its use.

Relevance must be an important aspect of our ministry methods.[6] People should not feel as if they are entering a museum when they come to church or worship every Sunday. In his book *The Post-Quarantine Church*, Thom Rainer wrote, "Churches cannot minister effectively using methods for a world that no longer exists."[7]

Ministry must be relevant with Christ at the center. Christ has called us to be creators and cultivators instead of curators. Therefore, the ministry must be attractive to introduce the culture to the gospel because the gospel message will not change, but the methods to present it have evolved since the coming of Christ. I believe that this is the aim of Paul's message to the church in 1 Corinthians 9:20-23. Paul wanted to win, and so should the church.

In 1 Corinthians 9:20-23, the apostle Paul speaks to meeting people where they are for the sake of the gospel. The goal is to present Jesus Christ in a fashion that relates to those he wants to evangelize. Paul could find points of commonality with Jewish Christians due to his heritage. Undoubtedly, he not only lived with them and dealt with them socially, but he deliberately followed Jewish practices dictated by the Mosaic law, even though it is not easy to explain specifically what these might have been from any of his writings.[8]

Paul could relate to those under the Law, and he tailored his message to help them see how the gospel is truth. Whereas he once lived as one under God's law, as it was given to Israel by Moses, he then saw himself legally bound in some sense to Christ.[9] He continued the logic in his argument, speaking in terms of the weak and the strong. Paul was flexible in his approach to share the gospel. He was neither rigid not parochial in his methodology and mindset to evangelize.

Paul recognized that salvation in Christ is both for the Jew and the Gentile, so he related the message in a way that was palatable to his audience. He did not discriminate as to who could receive the gospel. Implied is his love and concern for the salvation of all, no matter what their social or ethnic condition or religious conviction may have been.[10] His goal was to win all for Christ. In order to do so, Paul reasoned that his presentation must be relatable and relevant.

The power of ministry is in its presentation and relatability. Whether some have accepted this truth or not, the times in which we live are constantly changing. The same notion applies for relevant ministry.

Churches must come to the realization that our methodologies and practices must be current. We cannot function in the same capacity as we once did at the turn of the century and expect those who are unchurched to be attracted to God's church. Ministry must move with the times to ensure the survival of the local church. This is vital because generations that are being raised have a different perspective on everyday living.

For instance, my children live in a world where they communicate mostly through devices. For them, the telephone is a mini-computer in which they are accustomed to video-chatting. They relate speaking to their grandparents with seeing their images as well as hearing their voices. A phone call means Facetime. This was not the case ten years ago. So, if they are being reared in a world with these luxuries, what does it mean for a ministry that does not take these truths into consideration?

It speaks to the profound words of Jesus Christ: "And no one pours new wine into old wineskins. Otherwise, the wine will burst the skins, and both the wine and the wineskins will be ruined. No, they pour new wine into new wineskins" (Mark 2:22, NIV).

In the advent of the coronavirus pandemic, we witnessed many ministries burst. They were ill-prepared to handle such a grave shift in society. They had no infrastructure nor insight into sustainable ministry. When the pandemic hit, they were left to hold service solely via a teleconference line.

Unfortunately, some ministries closed their doors. If the leadership of the ministry had sought to be relevant, they could have kept their congregations connected, even if they were unable to meet in person. Still, I believe that an opportunity was missed.

I am not saying this as an attack on the local church whose normal Sunday attendance is small. I know of many ministries whose congregational size is less than 50 members, but their ministry continued to thrive in the pandemic. These ministries have pastoral leadership that stresses the importance of relevant ministry. These leaders recognize that our church has entered a new era of existence with the same God.

The approach does not have to be as sophisticated as some would imagine. The formula could be as simple as a smartphone with a stand and an internet connection. Those ministries that were unafraid and unashamed to use technology and move with the times were able to stay connected in a way that was safe, thus minimizing the risk of exposure to the coronavirus. For some, worship in this way may not be the ideal means to gather, but it is relevant and practical. Worship in the new normal accelerated the quest for relevant ministry and provided an opportunity to evaluate the efficiency and effectiveness of ministry practices. It proved the importance that if the church desires to thrive, it must have a virtual ministry.

Virtual ministry is fluid, and leaders must be able to adapt quickly and often. In the quarantine church, we discovered that worship in the virtual space could not mimic the worship when people are present in the sanctuary. Some elements of the worship service had to go because they were not functional in the virtual space.

When we began worship in the pandemic, we thought we could mirror our customary practices. The only problem is that our customary practices were so heavily dependent on people. For example, our call-and-response liturgies, the corporate welcome that we call our "holy hug," and the altar call could not be practiced as usual. It was alarming to me and my church how conditioned we were to what we considered church. COVID worship forced us to reevaluate our services, and we made key changes.

We eliminated the need for multiple people to be present in the sanctuary for worship, including our music staff and volunteers. We felt that it was best for our worship team to remain at home. Because we could not control where people traveled and ventured during the week, the safest and healthiest option was to have our worship team explore new ways to present music in worship. This enhanced our creativity in the worship space. We discovered different gifts and skills within the congregation. With the help of technology, we created a virtual choir.

We continued an element of live worship: preaching. Every Sunday, I continued to preach live from our worship center. We streamed the recorded portion of our music as a video uploaded to YouTube and played it from our worship center. When the music concluded, our media person cut to me to preach the sermon live. I chose to preach live to present some sense of the worship service that would be familiar to our congregation. Preaching on Sunday helped me maintain my routine of preparation that did not disrupt precious time with my family.

Virtual worship enhanced my approach to leadership that coincided with our ministry continuum. It is another means for us to fulfill our vision and mission. Listed below is an example of how the virtual ministry space helped fulfill the vision and mission of Shiloh.

Shiloh Baptist Church of Alexandria, Virginia

The vision of Shiloh Baptist Church of Alexandria, Virginia, is to be one church, actively advancing the kingdom of God. Our mission is to spread the message of faith, hope, and love in Jesus Christ by equipping disciples to engage the community locally and globally for the purpose of advancing the kingdom of God. We developed our vision and mission statement by surveying the congregation as to what type of ministry they want to be. Overwhelmingly, they spoke of the commissions of Christ in the Gospel of Matthew 28:18-20 and in Acts 1:8.

The kingdom of God is the reign of God in the lives of His people, where Jesus Christ is Lord and King in our lives. It is His Holy Spirit working in us, through us, and around us so that we live and do the will of God as God intends.[11] In the kingdom of God, we recognize that the church of the living God holds the responsibility of spiritual formation of its members.[12]

Spiritual formation is the gradual development of the heart of God in the life of a human being, aided by contemplative prayer, inclusive community, and compassionate ministry. The task of spiritual formation is actualized

through its mission to fulfill the *vision*. The vehicle that we use to achieve the aforementioned is evangelism. Essentially, *evangelism* is how we carry out the mission to fulfill the vision. Our goal is to be externally focused and internally strong. We will operate with a three-pronged approach: Engage, Equip, and Evaluate.

Ministry Continuum

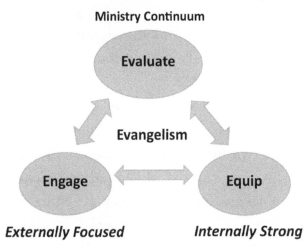

Ministry Continuum

This responsibility leads to an ongoing evaluation of the ministry so that we continually engage the community and equip disciples. Through this approach to ministry, we seek to fulfill the vision with the evangelistic premise that good deeds create goodwill, and goodwill creates the platform to see and share the good news.[13]

A virtual ministry presence should fit the vision and mission of our church. The pandemic helped us to envision this. As we continued to worship in the quarantine church, we discerned more of an opportunity and need for this platform of ministry to fulfill our vision.

Initially, when we began in the virtual space, I saw it as an evangelistic move to introduce people to Christ with the hopes that they, eventually, would come to our campus physically and join the ministry. The focus and goal were to get people into the pews. But during the pandemic, that became impossible and unwise. Given this truth, one thing became clear: The church could no longer be limited to a physical address.

The fact that people could not come to the campus illumined another reality: The digital, virtual, or online church would be the new normal. Logically, it made sense. Those who comprise the Millennial and Generation Z demographics are those who know and approach life from a digital perspective. Their everyday life is one lived with the internet and social media, not only as an option, but also as an intricate part of their daily existence.

If much of the world lives in this space, then this space is the field or sea where the church should be fishing,[14] and not only fishing, but living. This is a huge paradigm shift that we had come to realize. Virtual ministry had to be more than a tool for evangelism. It must become a way of life in the church, especially for any church that wants to make disciples. With this in mind, our ministry team emphasized the importance of evaluating our virtual ministry practices, especially our virtual worship experience.

One of the most—if not the most—important aspect of the virtual space (and ministry as a whole) is the evaluation of it. Through evaluation, I discovered more of the gifts and creativity present within our staff.

At our weekly staff meetings, we evaluate each Sunday worship service. Because worship solely in the virtual space was new to us, we increased our effort to constructively critique each service. This is where the creativity of the church staff flourished. We continued to use the evaluative practices of the ministry that is outlined in the book *The Externally Focused Quest* by Eric Swanson and Rick Rusaw. Swanson and Rusaw suggest that each ministry should ask the four following questions:[15]

- What is working? *Build on strengths that operate in regard to the mission.*
- What is stuck? *Identify problems or barriers we need to overcome to make progress of the mission.*
- What do we need to abandon? *Identify the activity that does not accomplish the mission. Everything has an expiration date, including ministry practices.*
- What could we try new? *Undertake initiatives to better fulfill the mission.*

These four questions guide our evaluation of the virtual Sunday service each week and have become a staple in our staff meetings. We take time to carefully hear everyone's thoughts and feelings around the worship service. On our staff, we have Boomers, Xers, and Millennials. Each person brings a different perspective that has proven to be beneficial and necessary to the improvement of our worship experience.

Through this evaluative experience, we have discovered more about our ministry via worship in the virtual space. The following list includes some aspects of the virtual church that have helped us shape and create a new worship culture at our church.

Eliminate the Fluff and Elements That Are No Longer Operative

In the virtual space, it would be unwise and impossible to replicate the pre-pandemic worship service. For obvious reasons, people would not be present. Due to the fact that most who watched would be in their homes, it was imprudent, if not irresponsible, to worship longer than 90 minutes. The attention span of worship in the home would not allow it.

We thought an overly long worship service would be a turn-off, too. Since every ministry with a virtual presence would be active on Sunday, the person seeking Christ may feel a sense of fatigue through a "Jesus overload" on Sunday, so our worship service must be proficient and succinct.

As a result, we moved from two live services to one. We introduced a new worship time at 10:00 AM. Prior to the pandemic, our church service lasted between 105 and 120 minutes. But our virtual worship experience is never longer than 75 minutes, with the average virtual service lasting 60 minutes. Listed below are some of the changes we made to make our worship experience succinct:

- We open the service with a five-minute countdown to worship (provided through the worship software Proclaim).

- We developed an intro worship song and video (video clips taken from an iPhone) that were written and produced in-house thanks to the giftedness of our worship team.

- We move to the worship song from some version of our virtual choir. (People record their part of the song prior to the service. We edit the video and then play it.)

- We then have the preaching, which is live from the sanctuary, followed by the invitation, appeal for the offering, announcements, and benediction.

In this time frame, we create moments to give, pray, and preach. We participate in the sacrament of Holy Communion and have encouraged people to use Communion elements from the church or provide their own. We have even produced Communion videos where we celebrate the occasion virtually with the virtual choir in community. We prepare a song of preparation and a concluding celebration.

In the staff meeting, we evaluate how we transition from one element of the service to the next. In our estimation, we believe that the sermon should take precedence in the service. The attendance in the virtual space is highest during preaching. (This was the case in pre-pandemic worship as well. Unfortunately, some parts of the worship culture do not change.)

In the virtual worship, you must be intentional about what and how you present Christ. You must get straight to the point. In the home, there will be other distractions and multiple responsibilities, so time is critical. We cannot deny or ignore that in today's culture, people have multiple options as to how they want to spend their time and to what they want to give their attention. Your presentation must be attractive and appealing to draw them in during a crisis to hear the good news about Christ.

Culture of Trust and Creativity

The evaluation process of our virtual worship service has created something beautiful: a culture of creativity among the staff. We devote the bulk of our staff meetings to ask the four aforementioned questions about worship. (What's working? What's stuck? What can we try new? What do we need to abandon?) As pastor, I try to make sure that every staff member's response is respected.

The fact that our staff represents three different generations is critical. They are a reflection of the demographics within the congregation. This truth has helped our ministry to be sensitive to the needs and perspectives of the worship audience. Every voice is valued, and all have contributed in amazing ways.

Much of how we do worship was birthed in the evaluative process of this experience. Through the evaluative process, we have created a culture of trust. I have witnessed us flourish as a cohesive team because we have created moments to dream, wonder, dissect, and discern.

Having a creative and supportive environment has produced a collaborative team that thrives.[16] This type of culture is a direct reflection of leadership. As pastor, you must create a culture where people and their voices are welcomed. They need to know that they matter and that their contributions will be recognized and rewarded. As the leader, you must create a space for your team to dream as you continually direct them to the vision and mission of the ministry. Creativity runs wild because people recognize the value in one another.

Our staff made creative suggestions that have enhanced our virtual presence. The ideas include what color schemes to use for the backgrounds of our countdown to worship, how we strategically place members on the screen in the virtual choir, how long we include the worship music for exaltation before the preached word, and when and where we place announcements.

This time has motivated the team to ask, What images are we presenting to the world, and what do these images speak about our ministry? My team helped to introduce and strategically place motion graphics in our worship. They have researched other products and technology to see if they are complementary to our worship culture.

Perhaps the greatest effort of creativity is in how we present and produce our worship music. Through this process, we discovered the gifts within our worship team.

Fortunately, we did not have to outsource production and editing for the virtual music and the choir. Everything we needed was in the house. By creating and cultivating a culture of trust and creativity, we unearthed the gifts within the ministry.

Creativity Yields Gifts Within the Ministry (What's in Your Hand?)

After the onset of the COVID-19 pandemic, the safest option for the health of the ministry was not to have worship personnel present in our virtual worship service. When I was led to make this decision, questions loomed large, in particular, How would we have music as part of our worship if the musicians and praise team were not present? I would soon learn that what we needed had already been provided.

Our minister of music, Kabanya Vinson, informed me that she would have conversations with some of her colleagues in ministry to ascertain how other churches were approaching worship. Additionally, I had conversations with our streaming provider and other pastors. Kabanya told me about a process that could not only enhance our worship, but that could help us virtually incorporate all music personnel in the worship experience.

The choir/ensemble could record themselves singing the selected song *a cappella*. They could do this by simultaneously singing along as they listened to the song through headphones. Then they would submit the video to the video editor, who happens to be our music director.

(He is a multi-hyphenate. He is our music editor, video editor, and special-effects technician.) He then would align all the videos and compile them into a video, where all of the choir participants would appear to be singing together in real time.[17]

Once we had a worship video that did not infringe on the safety of our congregation, we sought to employ a "virtual/live" model for worship. The worship service could be streamed live from the sanctuary, where preaching would be in real time, while the music ministry video would be played from the recording.

Initially, the music ministry video was quite raw and did not present the quality we had hoped for. So as a staff, we evaluated our worship service and continually worked to refine the process and implement tools to enhance the presentation. We were fortunate that most of what we needed was already in-house.

For instance, we now use a resource called Igniter Media. Igniter Media has a number of thematic graphic images, with colorful animated motion backgrounds, countdowns, and welcome and closing images, as well as motion graphics for our virtual worship video and tools that allow us to engage with the congregation. In our five-minute countdown to worship, we use Bible trivia questions that the congregation can answer while they wait for the online service to begin. Interestingly, we were already using Igniter Media before the pandemic. But given the virtual space for worship, we discovered that we were not using all of its tools and resources.

The virtual worship experience compelled us to look deeper into all of our existing resources and discover their full functionality. The same was true of our worship platform, Proclaim. Additionally, our music/video editor has found many plug-ins that he uses in Final Cut Pro, an Apple editing software that adds amazing special effects to each video. Every week, the videos are improving and are more creative. Again, the most amazing aspect of all of this is that the tools and gifts were already in our possession.

As a leader, it is important to continually take stock of your congregation and discover the gifts that God has placed in your midst. In the body of Christ, gifts are bestowed and given freely to believers. Often, people are waiting for an invitation to serve. Even if you have an abundance of resources and capital at your disposal, it is a good idea to invite people who are part of the congregation to participate. They are more prone to have the care and passion for the church. There is a sense of ownership they embody that flows from your expectations of them. That is, they take the spirit of your approach to ministry.

I have discovered that it is much easier to work with people who are part of the culture and environment I have established and cultivated. The lesson I continually learn is that the Lord provides what is needed to move forward if we have the faith and patience to discover it. This notion also bodes true for our digital platforms and streaming.

Digital Platforms and the Courage
to Stay Connected

We looked for ways to keep people encouraged during the pandemic. The desire to do this created an environment for newness. We actively sought to do things differently. We met multiple times with our streaming provider, LifeStream TV, to see what options were possible. We discovered that with our streaming URL and stream key, we could access multiple platforms to stream our content.

In the pre-pandemic church, we streamed our services via our website, YouTube, Facebook Live, Roku, and Twitter. We wanted our reach to go wide and far, so we added AppleTV and Amazon FireTV to increase our virtual presence. But there was one caveat: All of our streaming was done from the sanctuary of our worship center, and now we needed the ability to do this from home.

In our weekly meetings with our streaming provider, I was exposed to many applications and multimedia software in the marketplace that could facilitate our hopes and dreams. We chose to use the Zoom platform because of its familiarity. We discovered that from one Zoom account, we could stream content to all of our platforms.

I now conduct our Tuesday Night Teaching from home. With the livestream option on Zoom, we are able to stream to our existing worship platforms. The same is true with Larix, a multimedia application for mobile devices that allows us to stream from a tablet or a phone. Our streaming host informed us that we could go live to our platform at any time. All we needed was the URL and the streaming key. Once we had these two items, we could stream to multiple platforms from a number of media applications.

Learning all of these technical aspects of worship was, and still is, eye-opening. To know that I could transmit communication at anytime from anywhere to the congregation was priceless. Pastorally, this would do wonders for me to have the ability to have multiple ways to touch the congregation without being restricted or confined to one space or medium.

There are a host of streaming companies, such as LifeStreamTV (our provider), ChurchOnline, Boxcast, DaCast, Sermon Cast, and Streaming Church TV—just to name a few. (But be sure to do your research to see what fits your culture.) Also, there are multiple media platforms geared toward meetings, such as Adobe Connect, WebEx, Microsoft Teams, StreamYard, and Skype. We have used other digital technology to keep the church connected as well.

During the Lenten season, we used Text-in-Church. This is a service that helps us communicate with our first-time guests and visitors. A guest can text "Hello" to a number, and our ministry communicates with them for the next eight weeks. During the pandemic, we use this digital service for our congregation and for anyone who views our worship service and wants to send prayer requests. They simply text "pray" to the same number. The prayer goes to our intercessory prayer ministry, which continues to meet weekly via our Zoom platform.

For 21 days of the Lenten season, our church received an encouraging and inspirational message each morning by texting the word "hope." Some of our members who were grieving the loss of loved ones or who were in chemotherapy for cancer treatment informed me how the daily inspirational messages kept their faith alive. This 21-day digital devotional is another means to keep people engaged and connected to the ministry. The crux of the matter is that in the digital space, there exist a myriad of means to do ministry.

The virtual worship space has transformed our ministry tremendously. We discovered so much about the abilities of our staff and team. Through our attempt to provide excellent ministry in the digital space, God revealed the gifts of people within the ministry, increased our patience, and improved our tolerance to try something new. This pandemic has illuminated the truth that with God all things are possible (Matthew 19:26). It has fostered unity among our staff and inspired us to dream big.

Pastors and leaders, perhaps what you need is already in the congregation. You have members with gifts, talents, and ideas who are ready to help; they just want to be asked. Now is the time to engage your church and the community who is willing to assist you in your quest to be relevant.

The digital space and aspects of worship are not going to expire. They will only be enhanced as new technology is birthed daily. It is a matter of you moving out of your comfort zone to comprehend and consider how you can reach the world for Christ. You must employ multiple approaches while maintaining a central message that Jesus Christ is Lord.

Do not be afraid to cast your nets wide to reach a diverse sea within humanity to win the world for Christ. Let the digital world be your harvest to gather. Then, seek to make disciples in and through the countless methods that exist at your disposal.

As a leader, it would behoove you to anticipate members and guests to remain at home on Sunday as the pandemic eases and we return to the sanctuary. You cannot expect that everyone will be in a rush to come back to the building. Therefore, you should employ a hybrid, which is a both/and strategy, and consider how to make disciples through worship in the home because worship in the home is where we turn next.

Leader Examination

- At the beginning of the pandemic, did you consider your ministry to have a virtual presence? If so, how has it improved? If not, what changes have you made?

- What have you learned about ministry in the COVID pandemic? What has made your worship experience unique in the pandemic?

The Pandemic Pastor

- Do you feel that you are leading a relevant ministry? If so, what about the ministry makes it relevant? What are the practices in your ministry that you will consider eradicating to remain relevant?

- How has the pandemic helped you shape or reshape your vision?

- How do you evaluate your worship service and ministry? Would you consider your ministry to have a culture of trust?

- Are you certain of your gifts, talents, and abilities as a leader? Do you know the gifts of the people in your congregation or institution? How have you helped to identify the gifts of the people in your congregations?

Prayer for Pandemic Pastors and Leaders:

God, You are the Creator. I am made in Your image, which means that creativity is in me. Lord, call forth the creativity from within me as I yield to You, the God who makes all things new. Help me not to become complacent or lazy in my approach to my worship through my service and ministry to You.

Reveal to me the people, companies, and organizations that can help propel Your vision forward. Grant me the courage to do a new thing that is in alignment with Your will and way for my life. Help me to discern when and where

You are moving so that I can stay in step with You. Help me to be secure in who You called me to be so that I can receive constructive criticism from those I serve alongside.

Let Your Spirit reign in my speech, and help me to see people as You see them. Grant me the wisdom to develop a culture of trust within the team and organization, and help me to see the value and humanity of everyone I encounter on my way to fulfill Your will for me. Grant me the words to speak so that others will hear sincerity and comfort in my words as I seek to please You. In the name of Jesus, I pray. Amen.

[1]Nona Jones, *From Social Media to Social Ministry* (Grand Rapids: Zondervan, 2020), 7.

[2]"In US, Decline of Christianity Continues at a Rapid Pace," Pew Research Center, October 17, 2019, http://www.pewforum.org/2019/10/17/in-u-s-decline-of-christianity-continues-at-a-rapid-pace/.

[3]George Barna and David Kinnaman, *Unchurched* (Carol Stream, IL: Tyndale Momentum, 2014), 8-9.

[4]Ibid, 20.

[5]Nona Jones, *From Social Media to Social Ministry*, 7.

[6]Ibid, 8.

[7]Thom Rainer, *The Post-Quarantine Church* (Carol Stream, Ill: Tyndale Momentum, 2020), 37.

[8]J. A. Fitzmyer, Vol. 32, *First Corinthians: A New Translation with Introduction and Commentary* (New Haven; London: Yale University Press, 2008), 369.

[9]Ibid, 370.

[10]Ibid, 372.

[11]Gene Mims, *The Kingdom Focused Church* (Nashville: B&H Publishing, 2003), 40.

[12]Henri J. Nouwen, Rebecca Laird, and Michael Christensen, *Spiritual Formation* (New York: Harper One, 2010), 5.

[13]Eric Swanson and Rick Rusaw, *The Externally Focused Quest* (San Francisco: Jossey-Bass, 2010), 161.

[14]Nona Jones, *From Social Media to Social Ministry*, 10.

[15]Eric Swanson and Rick Rusaw, *The Externally Focused Quest*, 208.

[16]Sam Chand, *Leadership Essentials* (Sam Chand Leadership Institute, 2018), 40.

[17]Kabanya Vinson, Interview, May 27, 2021.

CHAPTER FOUR

SACRED SPACE OF WORSHIP IN THE HOME

"Every day they continued to meet together in the temple courts. They broke bread in their homes and ate together with glad and sincere hearts, praising God and enjoying the favor of all the people. And the Lord added to their number daily those who were being saved." (Acts 2:46-47, NIV)

DURING the pandemic, the virtual church has transformed worship and the concept of sanctuary. It has given new meaning for entering His gates with thanksgiving and His courts with praise. The sanctuary or the temple has been the central place where the people of God gather to worship the Lord. Much planning and resources have been dedicated to ensure that the sanctuary is well-kept or, at the very least, functional. For most of us, the concept of sanctuary and sacred space is the church building. Most traditional churches are attached to a building, and such is the case in my context.

Our worship center, located in Old Town Alexandria, is our current sanctuary. It is a transformed warehouse. The church began worshiping there in 2005, ten years before my arrival as pastor, and its seating capacity is 650. But it is the historic sanctuary that is synonymous with the name *Shiloh* in Alexandria. The historic sanctuary was built in 1893, and it was the church's second sanctuary due to the fact that the first one was destroyed by a fire in 1872. The people of Shiloh have a deep affinity for the historic sanctuary located on Duke Street. It was here that the majority of the congregation met Jesus. Their faith, fellowship, and community are inextricably linked to this place.

Like many churches in my context (the African American diaspora), worship in a central location is a primary ingredient of Shiloh's ecclesial identity. In the African American religious tradition, "worship is more experiential than rationalistic."[1] In this experience, Christians meet a risen Savior who is concerned with their individual and collective plight.

Across denominational lines, African American Christians engage in worship to "offer thanks and praise to God in and through Jesus Christ, and to be spiritually fed by the Word of God."[2] This worship happens at the building. This church as a people, and the building in an African American community, are viewed as a safe haven.

Historically, the African American church represented a safe space of refuge where Christian faith was actualized to affirm and nurture black humanity in a demeaning social existence.[3] The church was and continues to be the place where African American Christians "steal away" to renew their faith in God. This practice remains true for Shiloh. Even given its challenges historically, Shiloh remains a safe haven and a temporary escape from the troubles in the world.

Traditionally, the church has been the center of social life in the African American community.[4] Moreover, just as Alexandria once represented a haven for enslaved people in bondage, Shiloh has been a place of refuge and freedom for worshipers who continue to experience oppressive behavior in society. Since its inception, African American churches have been a community and a place of liberation. These churches have existed as "therapeutic institutions fostering a culture of psychological freedom, mental health, and self-esteem."[5]

Beginning with the religious experience of those who were enslaved, the Christian religious experience in this community is uniquely African American, one that we can claim as our own. Thus, one can see how our building is so important to the community. It is the place where the people gather to love God and be loved by God. But the pandemic has challenged the ordinary life and culture of worship in the building.

At the height of the pandemic, it was simply not safe to gather in a building to worship. Ironically, our safe house and traditional place of refuge became unsafe. State mandates restricted mass gatherings and recommended the number of people who could safely gather at one time. (In Virginia, the number went from ten people to 50.) The main priority for the restrictions was public health.

So, we decided that it would be unwise to continue church in the same manner when the everyday normal had shifted to masks, social distancing, and hand sanitizer as a precious commodity. The church building had transformed into a large uninhabited space simply because it was unhygienic and irresponsible to commune as we were accustomed to doing so. We began worship in the pandemic with an intimate number of our worship team (less than 15) to record worship, while we livestreamed the service. But it became difficult for us to socially distance in worship, especially for the musicians and the audiovisual team.

The arrangement of the instruments had to change, but our media team could not socially distance properly. So, the staff made the decision to go virtual with the music portion of worship, while we livestreamed the preaching. Although a portion of the service occurred in our worship center, the people worshiped in their homes. This gave a new or a renewed meaning to the word *sanctuary* as the place of worship.

During the pandemic, the home has become, has been reemphasized, and has been repurposed as the gathering place for worship. In this light, the New Testament church in America has revisited a culture of worship in some aspects similar to the New Testament church of first-century Jerusalem as outlined in the Book of Acts. The early church met in their homes, which served as their sanctuary and safe haven.

The early church did not have church buildings in which to gather. As Acts 2:46-47 states, they met in the Temple courts daily. There was a twofold purpose. First, they remained faithful to their Jewish heritage by observing the Jewish hours of prayer at the Temple.[6] Since the Temple courts were the gathering spot of society, it was important for the believer to be where the people were.

Second, the early church carried an enthusiasm and a zeal for witness. It was for evangelistic purpose that they came to the Temple courts. However, the homes of the believers were the intimate places for worship. They celebrated the Resurrection in their homes. The breaking of the bread refers to the celebration of the Lord's Supper.

There was no one building in which to gather and celebrate the liturgy of the faith. The church was guided by the ever-present Holy Spirit, who shaped the early Christian community.[7] Because of this truth, the Holy Spirit could reveal itself at anytime and anywhere. Moreover, the Holy Spirit, the presence of the omnipresent God, is never constricted to one building.

God is the Creator, and He has never been restricted nor relegated to a building. Wherever the presence of the

Lord is, that place is a sanctuary. God said through the prophet Isaiah, "This is what the LORD says: 'Heaven is my throne, and the earth is my footstool. Where is the house you will build for me? Where will my resting place be? Has not my hand made all these things, and so they came into being?' declares the LORD" (Isaiah 66:1-2, NIV).

Because the earth is the Lord's (Psalm 24:1), God can be worshiped anywhere. God's dwelling place is the hearts of those who welcome the Holy Spirit into their lives (1 Corinthians 3:16). Sunday morning in the church building is a time of worship in community, but it is not the only place where God can be exalted.

During this pandemic, the home has become the sacred space of sanctuary and is the gathering spot for the people of God to worship virtually. The home should be a safe haven and a place of refuge for anyone, especially those who believe in Christ.

Home is the place where we spend a majority of our time. During the pandemic, the home has become the office building and the schoolhouse for many families. Corporations are seeing the benefit due to the reduction of the overhead costs of real estate for business. The truth is that the home has become a multipurpose space, but the home should still remain a safe and sacred space for worship of God in a pandemic or in the new normal.

A number of churches were livestreaming their services before the onset of the COVID-19 outbreak because some of the larger churches understood the need to do so for evangelistic purposes. They saw livestreaming as a way to extend the reach of the gospel. While it was once convenient to worship at home, now it is imperative. And for many, it is the only option to worship. Churches who had a technological platform for streaming and communication were ahead of the curve and well-equipped to handle the transition, but now it has become necessary for survival.

The pandemic should force pastors and leaders to rethink everything. Yes, that even means worship. Home is the place for worship and should continue to be the place for worship. The principles and precepts of Christ and the practice of prayer and meditation should be magnified in the home. The love of God must be authentic first in the home. The pandemic has given the church an opportunity to reevaluate its religious practices and discover how worship in the home is paramount to the life of the church.

Wise pastors will understand that a return to normal is impossible because the pandemic has forced a new normal upon us. The church will be an amalgamation of the former and the new in its desire to be relevant. The digital world is upon us and thriving, and the body of Christ must adjust. What is more, the community can still gather in the home together with glad hearts.

At Shiloh, one of the ways we changed our approach to worship is to ensure that the home should become a central gathering space for the body of Christ. This is not a neglect of the brick-and-mortar church building, but more of a repurposing and an openness for its uses. Since the home has now become the sacred space for worship, our worship practices should consider this truth.

Just as the early church gathered with glad hearts in the homes of believers, we too should do likewise. Sunday morning worship is the gathering in multiple locations with the purpose to exalt the Lord. We should approach this hour in our sacred space with reverence. Worship in the home has helped reset and reestablish the Lordship of Christ in one's life. It helps the believer further understand the truth that the Holy Spirit is not confined to one location. Christ is Lord at every moment and everywhere.

In order to emphasize this notion, we created multiple times to stream our service. We understand that everyone may not be able to tune in at the same time. To make this convenient, we offered the worship service multiple times on Sunday.

Some of our members are essential workers, and they could not log on at 10:00 AM. We rebroadcasted the service at 1:00 PM and 6:00 PM. But worship in the home is not restricted to the 60- to 75-minute once-a-week service on Sunday. It is continuous. As pastor, I had to discover ways to foster home worship during the week to ensure that discipleship continued. Here are some strategies that helped us:

Morning Prayer

Prayer is the essential element and practice for believers, and it has been instrumental in the life of our ministry. The people of God are called to pray. It was important for us during the pandemic for the congregation to pray. Given the intensity of grief due to COVID-19 deaths of family members and the swift change of normal life, the community of believers needed to gather for prayer and seek God. The pandemic has forced many churches, in particular pastors, to focus on prayer.

For the last five years, we have prayed at noon each Wednesday for what I called a Prayerscope, where the church gathered on Periscope to pray. But our church needed more. Our intercessory prayer team continued to pray once a week, but we needed even more prayer. At the outset of the pandemic, our ministerial staff prayed twice each week (Wednesday and Sunday) at 6:00 AM, but I felt a call and an instruction for more prayer that was inclusive of the entire congregation. So, at the beginning of the year, we started a more intense life of prayer.

At the beginning of each year, the church participates in a Daniel Fast. For 21 days, we eat vegetables only and drink water or juice only (Daniel 10:3-4). We produce a 21-day devotional guide, along with certain recipes that adhere to the restrictions of the fast. For 2021, I decided to go live on our worship platforms at 6:00 AM each morning for prayer and devotion. For 21 days, we prayed together as a church via the Zoom platform that streamed live (Lifestream) to our worship platforms (our website, You-Tube, Facebook Live, and Periscope/Twitter).

Also, we used a teleconference line from Freeconferencecall.com. Our prayers were focused on our core values, "Be W.H.O.L.E.," which stands for Worship, Healing, Obedience, Love, and Empowerment. This time of prayer was transformational and well-attended. We averaged between 100 and 120 each morning. The enthusiasm around prayer was so powerful that once the fast concluded, we decided to continue to assemble together for prayer at 6:00 AM twice a week (Wednesday and Sunday). The engagement has been consistently strong.

During Holy Week 2021, we prayed each morning at 6:00 AM (akin to what we did during the Daniel Fast) and concluded the Holy Week prayer with a 6:00 AM virtual Sunrise Resurrection Service. (This service is a tradition we continue to celebrate.) Praying together as a church in the home connected us with the worship practices of the first-century church. Prayer as a church in community increased our dependence on God. It has helped us maintain our devotion and fellowship, and it is the one practice of the church that has provided an environment for discipleship to flourish.

Leaders within the church have testified that our corporate and communal prayer in the morning has sharpened their focus, centered their emotions, and increased their dependence on Christ. Other leaders have testified that corporate prayer has deepened their understanding of submission to Christ.

Whatever the culture of your ministry, I implore you to underscore the importance of praying together as a church. Ask your congregation how you can pray together. Take advantage of technology via social media outlets and teleconference lines. The health of your church will depend on the priority you place on prayer. You must seek the Lord as well as discern the culture of your church to know how often you need to pray. Know this, Scripture proves that there is power when the church prays together (Acts 2:1-4; 12:5; 16:25).

I am appealing to pastors to make prayer the essential spiritual discipline in your life personally as well as corporately with the congregation. Prayer makes a difference, and prayer works.

Discipleship Is Critical

A critical area for worship in community is that of discipleship. Since the home is now the central place for worship, ministries must cultivate an environment and employ methodologies for relevant discipleship. When we speak of discipleship, we are referring to the process by which the believer participates in community to be sanctified or made holy. This is the shaping and fashioning into the character of Christ by growing in the knowledge and grace of our Lord and Savior.

But discipleship does not happen in a vacuum. It flourishes and is developed in community. One way to ensure this is to make sure the interpersonal engagement of developing disciples is fostered through ministry. The ministry must create opportunities for this to happen, and it is charged to so do regardless of the atmosphere. It is important to note that life transformation does not happen automatically, nor does it develop via osmosis by attending one service a week.[8] It never has. The Jesus model of discipleship was intentional and interpersonal.

Discipleship must be a transformative and progressive process by which the ministry promotes a self-directed, self-governing obedience to the word of God that yields a hunger for righteousness for the congregation to share its faith through a wholistic lifestyle.[9]

Perhaps thinking about discipleship from a virtual space was the most critical aspect of the virtual church. The pandemic created an opportunity for us to witness this paradigm shift more closely. It helped us see the need to alter our strategy. We learned that we could be relational in the virtual space and create different opportunities for discipleship to manifest. Thus, it was critical for us to envision ourselves as a social ministry and not one that merely uses social media.

In her book *From Social Media to Social Ministry*, Nona Jones explains the difference: "A social media plan focuses on getting people to the building for a couple of hours every weekend, whereas a social media ministry strategy focuses on how to help them grow in their faith through social technology after they leave. You need both, and if you focus only on a social media plan, you will build an audience while stopping short of building disciples."[10]

The charge from the Lord is to go and make disciples of all nations (Matthew 28:18-19). The nations are in the digital space. This is where we must travel to make disciples. Discipleship is not a marketing technique, nor is it simply having a virtual presence. It is relational. Therefore, it is of utmost importance for any pastor to lead ministry centered on discipleship, relationally. The question is not, Why discipleship? But, How do we facilitate discipleship within the pandemic, and how should we continue discipling post-pandemic?

We discovered that corporate prayer via our worship platforms was one medium to help foster discipleship in community in the sacred space of the home. Another is our corporate Bible study known as Tuesday Night Teaching (TNT). Bible study has been a staple in our ministry. Like our Sunday worship services before the pandemic, we would livestream it. Attendance was sporadic. Customarily, we would have no more than 25 to 30 people in the sanctuary (not encouraging for a 1,000-member congregation). Our streaming numbers were low as well.

However, at the onset of the pandemic, this number changed. When we went virtual with TNT, our attendance increased 200 percent! Seeing this dramatic rise in participation, I decided to use this format for the near- and long-term future, and the demographics of our congregation support this approach. Although our church is located in Alexandria, Virginia, our church serves members who live in two states and the District of Columbia. We are a commuter congregation where most members live at least 20 to 30 minutes from the church campus, barring traffic.

Simply, it is more convenient to meet in homes for Bible study, so we chose to use the Zoom video platform that delivered Bible study to all our worship platforms (Lifestream, YouTube, Facebook Live, and Roku). Facebook Live is ideal for those who have a desire to interact with the teaching through questions and comments. Members have shared that they are growing in their relationship with God and have developed a higher sensitivity to the aegis and guidance of the Holy Spirit.

All of our Christian education offerings and life classes continued to use Zoom for ministry, including our Shiloh U Sunday school and new-member orientation, as well as our ministry meetings. But the most impactful ministry via virtual discipleship has been our children's ministry.

Our normal children's church used to meet at 11:00 AM on Sundays during our second worship service. Parents would drop off the children in the multipurpose room and then proceed to the sanctuary. But in the virtual space, we didn't feel that parents and children could worship simultaneously at home. Besides, we deemed that the worship experience on Sunday morning should be inclusive of the entire family.

Since we had one worship experience on Sunday at 10:00 AM, we moved the at-home children's worship to Saturdays at 10:00 AM. Parents have stressed to us the importance and blessing for their children to continue to worship together. Our attendance has ballooned 300 percent since the onset of Children's Zone.

Children between the ages of five and ten are actively engaged in worship. They worship, sing, and dance to YouTube clips from KidzBop. The sermonette or teaching from our Children's Zone teaching team is interactive via our platform. The children pray, read Scripture, and ask questions about the lesson. We have connected children across multiple states, while one trend has continued: Children have been the evangelists who ensure that their parents stay connected to ministry. They are the bridge that connects Christ to the home.

The same is the case for our youth. Our B3 student ministries (Be Empowered, Be Encouraged, Be Engaged) dedicated to middle and high schoolers continued to thrive during the pandemic. Before the pandemic, our B3 student ministries met for youth church twice a month (the second and fourth Sundays) at 11:00 AM.

Similar to how the children's church met pre-pandemic, the youth met while their parents were in service. But in the virtual space, we stressed the importance of family worship together as one church at 10:00 AM. So, the youth felt that Sundays at noon would be the optimal time for their worship.

Additionally, the youth gathered for Bible study and fellowship on Thursdays at 7:00 PM. They used Zoom for all their gatherings. The youth are so engaged that they took the lead on worship in the virtual space. Creatively, they have flourished in virtual worship by adding their own graphic effects to their videos. Our youth have thrived in this virtual space namely because it is a space to which they are accustomed.

Our life ministries continued to thrive as well. Our women's ministry exploded with growth and participation, and the attendance during our Discipleship Women's Month doubled. The same was true of our men's ministry. We continued *Authentic Manhood: the 33-Series,* in six-week increments for our discipleship. Our marriage ministry also thrived as we held quarterly gatherings that had consistent involvement.

The key for these ministries was the ability to interact and converse with one another. Every gathering was not didactic in nature. The conversations were guided by a facilitator and based on a theme. In every aspect, our goal was to create a space for people to be and to share.

The pandemic weighed heavily on the soul and psyche of humanity, but life did not stop. Amid the crisis, people continued to struggle with issues around family, marriage, children, and work. Our life ministries provided opportunities for pastoral care and compassion that help keep the church connected, although we could not gather in person. We emphasized the importance of the home and the sanctuary that has proven to be beneficial for the vitality of our church.

Worship in the home has transformed our church for the better, and this opportunity for ministry is exciting! Because of technology, our reach extends beyond the walls of a sanctuary. There will be members of the church who will choose the location as to how they desire to worship.

Thom Rainer suggests that the post-quarantine church will be comprised of the digital only, the digital transitioning, and the dual citizen.[11] In order to be effective and relevant, we must give attention to each demographic. In this light, worship at home in the pandemic has aided this approach.

Our leadership must be comfortable with the fact that people will join our fellowship and community without ever coming to our campus to worship. Churches who insist on being relevant will make the appropriate change to meet the needs of these members without neglecting others who choose differently. We must consider what ministry means to the entire congregation and not make preferential distinctions.

Nonetheless, discipleship must be at the core of our existence as a church. Remember, the key is to remain relevant, fluid, and open to the many possibilities present in the digital space. Be unafraid to try something new, especially since you serve a God who makes all things new (Revelation 21:4-5).

Leader Examination

- Do you consider the home to be a sacred space? How have you helped your congregation cultivate worship in the home?

- Has your approach to discipleship changed during the pandemic? If so, how? What nuances have you made to ensure that discipleship continues in your ministry?

- What elements of your ministry do you intend to keep and continue, even when in-person ministry activities are safe and acceptable?

- Do you consider your ministry to have a social media ministry or a social media plan? Are you investing resources or planning to maintain a social media ministry in a post-quarantine church?

Prayer for Pandemic Pastors and Leaders:

Lord God, You are God of the universe. You are Lord over the earth. Your Spirit is not confined to a building. You are Lord everywhere, and I desire that You be Lord of my home. I consecrate my home to be the place where You dwell. You are welcome in my home to rest, rule, and reign. Send Your angels to protect the premises of my home at all times. Grant me the wisdom to sense You in my home, and give me understanding about how to lead Your people in these times.

Help me to create innovative ways to disciple Your people. Create in me and in them a hunger to mature in You, and give me the strength not to be discouraged along the journey to lead a relevant ministry. Raise up leaders in community and congregation who are technologically savvy to help us stay connected in community as we seek to become whole in You. In the name of Jesus, I pray. Amen.

[1]Melva Wilson Costen, *African American Christian Worship* (Nashville: Abingdon, 1993), 18.
[2]Ibid, 13.
[3]Dale P. Andrews, *Practical Theology for Black Churches* (Louisville: Westminster John Knox, 2002), 34.
[4]Robert M. Franklin, *Crisis in the Village* (Minneapolis: Fortress Press, 2007), 108.
[5]Ibid, 109.
[6]C. K. Barrett, *A Critical and Exegetical Commentary on the Acts of the Apostles* (Edinburgh: T&T Clark, 2004), 170.
[7]J. B. Polhill, *Acts*, Vol. 26 (Nashville: Broadman & Holman Publishers, 1992), 121.
[8]Nona Jones, *From Social Media to Social Ministry*, 67.
[9]Nolan W. McCants, *The Digital Pulpit* (Monee, IL: 2021), 51-52.
[10]Nona Jones, *From Social Media to Social Ministry*, 13-14.
[11]Thom Rainer, *The Post-Quarantine Church* (Carol Stream, Ill: Tyndale Momentum, 2020), 31.

CHAPTER FIVE

MINISTRY INSECURITY AND THE IMPORTANCE OF CONGREGATIONAL CULTURE

"Nevertheless the people refused to obey the voice of Samuel; and they said, 'No, but we will have a king over us, that we also may be like all the nations, and that our king may judge us and go out before us and fight our battles.'" (1 Samuel 8:19-20, NKJV)

A natural response in crisis is to resort to what is familiar and comfortable, including bad habits and other elements of dysfunction. It is not natural to view a crisis as a time for opportunity. In crisis, we transition into survival mode, but something else happens. Crisis will expose how well-prepared you are and how well-structured your organization is. It will reveal the mental fortitude and aptitude within organizations. Churches will discover what works, what is worth holding on to, and what needs to be dismissed.

More important, the character of each leader will come to light. This is true in the church and, in particular, it is true for the pastor.

As the coronavirus pandemic gained strength, large gatherings were prohibited, including religious gatherings. For most churches, this meant that there could not be Sunday worship in the sanctuary. This was unfathomable! The one place where the doors were never closed is the church because it has usually been the central place of refuge in times of trouble.

Unfortunately, many pastors ignored the mandate to dismiss in-person worship, but their ignorance in leadership resulted in peril for the churches they led. Many people contracted the virus, and some of those people lost their lives because they attended church. The pastors who heeded the call to follow the ordinances and take safety measures now had to pivot and provide worship services in a different format, or at least churches had to expand their virtual worship experience and online presence.

The ministries that were operating in this space could transition easier than those that did not have the infrastructure to do so. Moreover, the demand for the technology to move into the virtual space was so overwhelming that it produced a backlog for available products. The demand exceeded the supply. So, if you did not have the infrastructure in place, you were behind the curve. Analogously, it was akin to a separation from the wheat and the tare.

Some pastors were prepared for the crisis, whether they recognized it or not. Those who put effort, energy, and enthusiasm into the virtual worship space were equipped to handle the demand for worship and keep the church connected, but another issue arose regarding the product or the presentation of the virtual space. Ministries that had the resources, finances, and capital to fund this kind of worship flourished, while other ministries struggled to stay afloat.

This problem exposed the worship culture of every ministry and called into question the competency of relevant leadership or the reality that resources, in particular financial resources, matter. Unfortunately, it revealed something else: a deeply embedded insecurity to become like other ministries instead of seeking God to establish one's own identity and ministry culture.

This problem of identity and insecurity as the people of God is not new. We see it with the children of Israel in their exodus from Egypt. When Yahweh sent Moses to Egypt to liberate the children of Israel from captivity, the seeds of insecurity were planted. Yahweh was fulfilling a promise made to Abraham regarding his descendants. After the plagues, the enslaved Israelites marched out of Egypt as a free people; but at the moment of crisis, they began to question the uncertainty of their future and their identity in God.

When adversity met Israel, their initial response to Moses was imbued with doubt: "They said to Moses, 'Was it because there were no graves in Egypt that you brought us to the desert to die? What have you done to us by bringing us out of Egypt? Didn't we say to you in Egypt, "Leave us alone; let us serve the Egyptians"? It would have been better for us to serve the Egyptians than to die in the desert!'" (Exodus 14:11-12, NIV).

This is how Israel responded at the hint of difficulty. When they were hungry, their insecurity spoke for them (Exodus 16:3). When they were thirsty, their reply was insecure (Exodus 17:3). When the spies were sent into Canaan to scope out the land Yahweh was giving them, they spoke from a position of uncertainty (Numbers 14).

Insecurity prevented a generation from inheriting God's promises. What is most disconcerting about Israel is the fact that when they complained, Yahweh answered and provided. Yahweh was there to give water, quail, and manna to satisfy their flesh. Moreover, when they complained as a liberated people standing before the Red Sea with Egypt in hot pursuit of them, Israel witnessed the power of God firsthand. They were the treasure that Yahweh moved to safety, and they saw how the Lord their God defeated Pharaoh's army.

However, the children of Israel were so bound by insecurity that they could not embrace the fact that the Lord was there with them and for them. Yahweh desired to shape their identity as the people of God, and He wanted to present them to the world as those who were a chosen people who would be the representation of the righteous on earth.

The children of Israel were the people of the sovereign God, but they could not see themselves as such. For them, it was difficult to accept who and how Yahweh was fashioning their unique sense of self. Israel desired to be something different than who God was calling them to be. Perhaps one moment in Israel's history signifies this nation's insecurity.

During the period of the judges (as recounted in 1 Samuel 8:19-20), the children of Israel asked Samuel the prophet, priest, and judge to grant them a king. They were tired of being a distinct nation. They had no craving to be different. In their eyes, value and prominence was to be like the surrounding nations who did not worship their God.

This word displeased Samuel and Yahweh: "But when they said, 'Give us a king to lead us,' this displeased Samuel; so he prayed to the LORD. And the LORD told him: 'Listen to all that the people are saying to you; it is not you they have rejected, but they have rejected me as their king. As they have done from the day I brought them up out of Egypt until this day, forsaking me and serving other gods, so they are doing to you. Now listen to them; but warn them solemnly and let them know what the king who will reign over them will claim as his rights'" (1 Samuel 8:6-9, NIV).

What was so fascinating about the other nations? What did Israel lack? Why were they enamored with the monarchial structure of leadership? In their request for a king, they rejected the Most High God as King! How could this be?

No earthly king harnessed the power to do what Yahweh had done for Israel down through the generations, so much so that other nations feared them because of their God. Israel was in a class all to themselves, but they were unable to recognize it. So, they aspired to mimic nations who worshiped false gods and idols because it was too uncomfortable to be different. They could not appreciate who God was to them and what God had done for them.

Moreover, the children of Israel did not understand that Yahweh had created a distinct culture through worship for His chosen people. Israel possessed its own identity but desired to discard it and mimic other nations who did not honor their God. Culture matters.

The struggle of identity in ministry that speaks to the culture of the local church was exacerbated during the pandemic. In ministry, in particular in leadership, there exists the tendency to do what works. When another ministry is successful at a certain program, ministry grouping, outreach event, or worship style, pastors want to copy what seems to be successful in another ministry.

There is nothing wrong with sharing strategies, tactics, or programs that have been successful. This is not to suggest that churches cannot learn from one another. We know the proverb as iron sharpens iron (Proverbs 27:17).

The problem is that what one ministry considers successful may be different from another. Often, the desire to repeat what another pastor, leader, or preacher is doing or has done happens at the expense of not consulting God. This can be detrimental to the church because pastors have yet to discern the culture of the ministries they lead.

Every ministry has its own DNA. There is an imprint of traditions, practices, and liturgy that has developed over time. History still resonates within the organization. Often, only a few know why ministries continue certain customs.

Essentially, every ministry has its own culture. The culture of an organization or an institution is its attitudes, behavior, and ways in which it functions and lives. Culture is about the systems and the people who execute and protect those systems. In his book *Cracking Your Church's Culture Code*, Samuel Chand regards culture as the personality of the church, which includes its tangibles and intangibles. It is the stated and unstated values, beliefs, and assumptions, how problems are handled, and how success is celebrated.[1]

Every church has a different culture because no one church is the same, just as no one person is the same. For instance, I share the same name as my father. In many ways, the imprint of his teaching and rearing is alive in me. Although I am his progeny, I have a different genetic makeup.

My wife is a twin. She and her sister share similarities, but they have different personalities. They are different people who approach issues, handle chaos, and solve problems through different means. They share the same parents, and before they were married they shared the same last name, but they are not identical.

And so it is with each ministry. No one church is the same, even if their racial and ethnic makeup is similar. We are all different. It is the same for the local church. Even though denominational ties may be the same, each congregation is not. To affect any type of change and transition to lead effectively with wisdom, pastors must exegete their congregations and understand their culture as well as discern the culture they want to create and cultivate.

This should be a continuous theological exercise of any spiritual leader. Conducting this practice with the guidance of the Holy Spirit will help stave off feelings and notions of insecurity. Embrace the truth that God has a unique purpose and design for you as a leader as you lead Christ's church. Thus, it is important to explore the concept of local theology. Local theology is a concept used for preaching, but I reason that it is most important for pastoral leadership.

Spiritual leaders must reflect critically and theologically concerning the congregation's culture. Knowing the culture of a congregation—its customs, traditions, and practices of a particular people within a specific context—is crucial for preaching, pastoring, and leadership. Culture affects doctrines and belief systems and provides the footing as to how people hear sermons and follow leadership.[2] An exegesis of the congregation must commence with an understanding of its culture. Each church has a unique culture concerning its worship practices. Therefore, pastors must employ a cultural hermeneutic to aptly ascertain the multiple dynamics that coexist in the life of the ecclesial community.

Every pastor preaches, minsters, and leads from within a particular social setting. Even Jesus of Nazareth existed in a specific living community in the world. The Rev. Dr. Kenyatta Gilbert, professor of homiletics at Howard University School of Divinity, suggests, "Jesus had a specific ethnic and religious identity . . . not separated from his Judaic heritage and social location."[3]

This conception that was true of Jesus is true for every pastor. Pastors are socially located within a specific context. Therefore, when they lead, they do so from within a certain construct that produces a contextual (cultural) hermeneutic. This concept is known as a "local theology."

The Reverend Dr. Lenora Tubbs Tisdale, the Clement-Muehl professor of homiletics at Yale Divinity School, suggests that preaching as local theology is "a highly contextual act of constructing and proclaiming theology within and on behalf of a local community of faith. It requires of the preacher interpretation of biblical texts, interpretation of contemporary contexts (including congregations and their subcultures), and the imaginative construction and communication . . . that weds the two in a fitting and transformative way."[4]

Preachers construct sermons and give leadership from a particular setting within a milieu of cultures and subcultures. Their own experiences and cultural lens intersect with a number of competing factors, for example, congregational context, tradition, experience, and biblical texts. Hence, the sermon is a theological invention of ecclesial, doctrinal, denominational, and traditional worlds that preachers bring together in an imaginative act with hopes for personal and communal transformation.[5]

But this is true of pastoral leadership and ministry practices as well. Each ministry has a preexisting culture that is accustomed to a particular style and function of proclamation and leadership. Therefore, congregational exegesis is a necessity for leadership.

Congregational exegesis is multifaceted. It is a necessary activity for any leader. Pastors and leaders must understand their own hermeneutical lens (self-exegesis) in addition to those within the congregation. They must be able to articulate their faith stories alongside the one within the congregation they lead. Congregational exegesis is a continual exercise of attentiveness where pastors scrutinize its life from multiple angles and levels.[6]

There are voices within the congregation competing for an audience that may contradict the voice of the pastor. Who are the influencers in the congregation? Who are the prominent families? The wise pastor should seek to become acquainted with the manner in which the people view and experience God. Exegeting the congregation involves observing, listening, and watching for symbols, idols, and landmines. An exegesis of the multiple symbols present in the congregation can only aid the pastor's sensitivity to the people.

A deep look at congregational exegesis seeks to answer the question, What is the "why" for the congregation? Since pastoral leadership has a goal of formation and transformation, one must be knowledgeable of how the congregation imagines and envisions God.[7] Pastors must ascertain what is sacred, whether that be architecture, vestments, programming, or style of worship.[8]

One of the hopeful outcomes of congregational exegesis is not merely obtaining information, but rather is the establishment of healthy and compassionate relationships between pastors and people. This will help ease the tension when any type of change is presented to the congregation.

Being pastoral within the congregation, spending intimate time with members, should foster love for them through humility. The humility is enhanced when pastors understand that this Christian community existed before their arrival. Pastoral leaders who are humble admit this truth as they seek to ascertain the brutal facts before deciding to act.[9] Knowing the history of a people creates an opportunity for compassionate relationships.

Furthermore, when pastors choose to operate as true shepherds to feed and lead their congregations, it fosters intimacy with God. Thus, spiritual leadership must originate and emanate from the space of love. Love is the basis for the hermeneutic that fashions leadership and shapes culture. Through love, pastors will discover what is amenable and what is plausible for their congregations.

Exegeting the congregation will inform you of the most efficient and effective process to enact change, but there are times when you must forge ahead for the sake of the overall health of the congregation. Your leadership teams may not see what you see. This could be God's orchestration so that you can build trust and dependency on God.

But, pastor, you must be unashamed to try! And if your new initiative does not work, do not view it as a failure. Instead, please review your steps and strategies to determine where you can improve. There are some things that have good intentions but simply will not work. This, too, is part of the exegesis process, but it is not an indictment that your ministry is less than or inept. Simply, what works for one ministry may not fit yours.

I discovered this early in my tenure as pastor. I was looking for a way to energize giving in the church, so I had discussions with other colleagues in ministry. One of my fraternity brothers who pastors a thriving congregation in Nashville informed me of some of his practices. At the beginning of each year, his church has a "Prove Me Campaign" (taken from Malachi 3:10) as a way to encourage tithing.

They call for those who have never tithed consistently as a practice to try to do so for 90 days. They even create a separate bank account to collect the tithes from these members, and they make a special promise. If those new tithers feel that God has not made a difference in their lives through this experience, the church will return the tithes to them. Yes, the church would give them a refund!

When I heard this, I bought into the entire concept. I spoke with the chair of the trustees, excited to bring this to my ministry, but she did not think that it would work. Why? Because she knew more concerning the culture of our ministry. At this time, I had only been senior pastor for 12 months. She agreed that we needed to do something to increase giving, but she could not see this as a means to do so. However, she agreed to try.

Needless to say, this method did not work for us. It was not that people did not desire to participate. I made the assumption that everyone in the congregation was educated about tithing, so I did not take time to understand patterns of giving and the faith approach of the congregation. This experience proves that knowing culture matters. This became even more evident at the onset of the pandemic. Simply, every approach cannot suffice for every ministry.

God has called each church to a specific purpose with a unique identity to serve a perfect God. To be a carbon copy of another ministry is a sign of unbelief and a rejection of God. That is like saying that God is not big enough to assign distinctively different purposes for each member and community within the body of Christ to meet specific needs and function in a particular way.

God can do the miraculous for those who believe and seek Him to ascertain His desires for His church. Every church cannot do everything well. This speaks to culture.

Israel possessed an inimitable culture that had been created through their relationship with Yahweh. Yahweh was the patient and compassionate God who delivered them from Egyptian captivity. He called them to be a holy people set apart from all the other nations on earth.

Israel was the chosen people who would be God's representatives in the world. Yahweh instituted their religious practices and customs because the Lord God wanted to shape and fashion their identity in Him. Yahweh understood that He had to establish them as a nation that had been liberated. Thus, He had to eradicate the culture they developed in Egypt as slaves and create a new culture as a liberated nation.

This was Yahweh's hope from the time of Moses through the period of the judges. Israel carried an exclusive and matchless identity as the people of God under theocratic rule. Yahweh was God and King. However, when they asked to have an earthly king akin to the surrounding pagan nations, they were expressing an unappreciation for what God had done. Moreover, they did not inquire of God to discover His desire for them. Essentially, they did not understand their culture and sought to be a copy, not recognizing that the God of creation had made them an original.

Understanding and preserving culture is not an excuse to have irrelevant ministry nor stall progress. This attitude can lead to the death of the institution. But each ministry must find what makes it come alive and, more important, discover what Christ desires for a particular church.

As leaders, we must avoid trying to make our churches carbon copies of the church down the street or across the river. There is a uniqueness about the place where Christ has called you. You must seek God to find why and where He has planted you in His ministry. You must be clear as to how God requires you to lead and be relevant for the surrounding community and the world.

As pastors and leaders, we must be careful in our approach to ministry. Our ministry methods must be guided by the principle that the church belongs to Christ, who has a specific function for each ministry that He desires to fashion. No one local ministry is identical.

Since we are all one in Christ (Galatians 3:28), we must combat ministry insecurity. That is, we should not feel inadequate or less than because our ministry does not mirror larger ministries. Every ministry is different.

This is not to suggest that we should not want to improve or increase the resources so that we reach more people for the sake of the gospel. However, the issue should not solely be increasing the size of the ministry, but more so being and offering one that is relevant. God has the power to increase the size of any ministry, but the question every pastor must ask is, Why? Is my desire to reach more for Christ, or is it to satisfy my ego? Will a larger budget change my dependency on God?

Whatever it is, you must be sure to find security in who God created you to be and how God wants you to lead the ministry that He has granted you stewardship over. No church, no matter its vision or culture, belongs to the people. Remember, every church belongs to Christ. It is His body.

Leader Examination

- What is the DNA of your ministry (culture)? What is the culture of the ministry that predates you? How do they relate? How do they differ?

- Has your church culture evolved over time?

- Do you compare your ministry to others? If so, why?

- In your desire to be like another ministry, are you expressing ingratitude for what God has done and is doing in your ministry?

- How often do you engage in self-exegesis and congregational exegesis? Do you have a formula as to how you conduct this exercise? Who are the trusted people in your congregation who can help you?

Prayer for Pandemic Pastors and Leaders:

Lord God, I thank You for calling me to lead. I desire to be led by You. Open my eyes to see clearly how You crafted the ministry and organization I lead. Reveal to me the landmines in the organization before a change is made. Show me the history of Your people, and grant me wisdom to discern its culture.

Remind me that I am fearfully and wonderfully made in You. Help me to understand that I have no need to compare myself to another leader, church, or organization. Reveal to me the unique way You have crafted me and the ministry You have called me to lead.

I embrace the words of Your servant David that helps me find affirmation in You: "Truly my soul finds rest in God; my salvation comes from him. Truly he is my rock and my salvation; he is my fortress, I will never be shaken" (Psalm 62:1-2, NIV). Lord, You are my rock. I rest in You. My value and affirmation are in You. Thank You, Lord! In the name of Jesus, I pray. Amen.

[1]Samuel Chand, *Cracking Your Church's Culture Code* (San Francisco: Jossey-Bass, 2011), 3-4.
[2]Ronald J. Allen and Joseph R. Jeter Jr., *One Gospel, Many Ears: Preaching for Different Listeners in the Congregation* (Saint Louis: Chalice Press, 2002), 116.
[3]Kenyatta Gilbert, *Exodus Preaching* (Nashville: Abingdon Press, 2018), x.
[4]Lenora Tubbs Tisdale, *Preaching as Local Theology and Folk Art* (Minneapolis: Fortress Press, 1997), 38.
[5]Ibid, 39.
[6]Sally A. Brown and Luke A. Powery, "The Preacher as Interpreter of Word and World," *Ways of the Word* (Minneapolis: Fortress Press, 2016), 137.
[7]Lenora Tubbs Tisdale, *Preaching as Local Theology and Folk Art*, 57.
[8]Lenora Tubbs Tisdale lists seven symbols of exegesis of congregational exegesis. Furthermore, she speaks of discerning cultural identity, and congregational ethos often is developed via the manner in which the congregation handles crisis. See Chapter 3, "Exegeting the Congregation," in *Preaching as Local Theology and Folk Art*. Sally A. Brown offers a three-view approach to congregational exegesis in "The Preacher as Interpreter of Word and World" in *Ways of the Word*.
[9]Omar L. Harris, *The Servant Leader Manifesto* (Columbia, SC: Intent Books, 2020), 28.

CHAPTER SIX

THE PRIORITIZATION OF SELF-CARE AND THE PRACTICE OF SABBATH

"Aaron shall bring the bull for his own sin offering to make atonement for himself and his household, and he is to slaughter the bull for his own sin offering. . . . He shall then slaughter the goat for the sin offering for the people and take its blood behind the curtain and do with it as he did with the bull's blood: He shall sprinkle it on the atonement cover and in front of it." (Leviticus 16:11, 15, NIV)

HEN COVID-19 began to change life as we knew it, the world was forced to adjust. This included the church. Because it was unsafe to gather in large numbers, our staff went through a month of machinations regarding our Sunday worship experience and weekly ministry meetings before settling on a somewhat stable approach. I say "somewhat" because in the COVID/quarantine worship space, we have learned the importance of

117

flexibility and being fluid in ministry methods. Ministry tactics can shift, but the core message of Christ must remain the same.

Still, the ability to make adjustments and plan properly takes a lot of focus, attention to detail, and exploration to find the right fit for individual congregational culture, and it takes a lot of work. If diligence is a good leadership quality, then what is required for church leadership during the pandemic is diligence on steroids.

Even though the church I pastored had made strides in the improvement of our online presence and technology upgrades, enough to keep the ministry solvent, the need to improve our ministry presentation intensified during the pandemic. We had a foundation, but we needed to enhance our worship service. We were constantly in scramble mode to find the right formula suitable for these times. It took, and is taking, a lot of work.

We introduced new teaming concepts, shifted responsibility of personnel, and revised leadership roles. We had to shift modes of communication because we were not present in the office. We met constantly with our streaming providers as we explored new possibilities.

I met frequently with church officers and leadership to offer encouragement and keep the spirit of the congregation alive. For the first half of 2020, I felt as if I was on an adrenaline rush to keep things moving. And in the midst of this, my son was in kindergarten learning from home, and my toddler daughter was running the house.

Parenting in a pandemic is enough. Parenting while teaching and working seemed to be too much. My wife and I had multiple responsibilities trying to adjust to everyone being at home. By the end of the year, as COVID cases continued to rise, I tried to exhale. But it was difficult to do. I was spent. During this entire ordeal as I sought to take care of my family and to be faithful to the ministry, I forgot about one important individual: me.

Self-care is essential for everyone, especially pastors and leaders. You could easily perform, minister, and lead the congregation and make the ministry a priority, while you neglect the care necessary for yourself. You can become entrenched in the daily grind to the point where it becomes your world. And in a crisis, the need to feel that you must be present and be all things for the ministry is amplified.

But here is the truth: God only made one you, and He never intended for you to be all things to all people. The church existed before you and will exist when you are no more. Besides, if you do not care for yourself, you cannot be the best version of you. A healthy you will be the best you. Before you can go to the Lord on behalf of the people, you must go to Him on behalf of yourself.

In Exodus and Leviticus, the Lord gave Moses strict instructions regarding how the priesthood should appear before the Lord. The Lord gave intricate details regarding the attire and application of the order of the priesthood. Aaron, Moses' brother, was the first high priest of the congregation of Israel. In Leviticus 16:11, 15, the Lord informs Moses as to how Aaron should make atonement for the sins of the congregation once a year.

The Day of Atonement happened amidst the Feast of the Trumpets and the Feast of Tabernacles (Booths), which were all part of the Feast of the Ingathering. Yahweh required that the sins of Israel be atoned for each year. The high priest bore responsibility for this holy act of worship; but before Aaron made the atoning sacrifice for the nation, he had to take care of his sin and that of his family. Yahweh commanded Aaron to offer a bull as a sin offering for himself and his house before he could offer a goat as a sin offering for the people. He had to ensure that his sin was dealt with before he could mediate the sins of the nation before God.

Theologically, no priest is commanded to perform this act in the New Testament church. We have a Great High Priest who doubles as the lamb of God, Jesus Christ (Hebrews 4:14-16; 9:23-28), who has made the once-and-for-all sacrifice for the sins of the world. Thank God that we as priests do not deal with the blood of goats, bulls, rams, and lambs. This is a messy process, although ministry itself is messy.

The point of the Scripture for the purposes of self-care is that Aaron had to perform duties on behalf of himself first. Before he could go to God on behalf the people, he was instructed to care for himself. I believe that this concept is applicable to us in the modern-day church. Neglect of self is a germ that can become infectious if not treated.

As pastors and leaders, we have a tendency to put the health and care of the organization before our own health. But we must be in the best shape to ensure that we are present to fulfill God's call. Too often, we neglect our physical, emotional, spiritual, and mental health, thinking that we are living sacrificially unto God with the hopes that He will see our service and reward us.

Pastor, you can live a life of sacrifice for the greater good of humanity and ensure that you are your best you. Sacrificial service to God is not neglect of self. To live sacrificially is to think of others and give preference to them out of love (Romans 12:10). It is an attitude that is antithetical to being self-absorbed and only thinking of yourself and how you can be the primary beneficiary of whatever is offered.

As a servant leader, you cannot serve to your highest duty if you forsake the health of your being. A neglect of self can cause you to be irritable and irrational in the handling of the ministry you serve. You can become easily disturbed when the mess of ministry presents itself. Your response can create an unhealthy work environment that is uninspiring. Pastor, you must take care of yourself.

Ministry has a tendency to be chaotic, and in crisis the chaos is escalated. As leaders, we must be adamant and aggressive in our pursuits to manage chaos and create calm. Dr. Beverly Malone—chief executive officer for the National League for Nursing, a licensed clinical psychologist, and a psychiatric mental health nurse—reasons that there are three stressors in the journey of life: the inevitable, the imposed, and the chosen.

The *inevitable stressors* are the ones that are beyond our control. These are the normal trials of life that are unavoidable. They include death, family issues, taxes, and aging. These stressors are always present.

The *imposed stressors* are those such as the current pandemic. The COVID-19 pandemic is an unauthorized stressor that has come upon us that we all have to accept and deal with if we desire to survive. These include the events of life that someone audaciously gives to you and you audaciously accept. Dr. Malone believes that these stressors play upon our feeling that we need to be needed. We must discern whether these stressors taste, smell, and look like our stress.

The *chosen stressors* are those we willingly participate in. These stem from the relationships we choose to engage in as well as how we handle our work environment. These include the additional pressures we place on ourselves, including our reactions to our disappointments and those in the world, what causes we give ourselves to and why.[1]

At times, these stressors are inextricably linked. They can act together simultaneously, and it can be difficult to discern which one is dominant. For pastors and leaders, these dynamics point to a question we must all ask. It is the same question that medical professionals must ask daily: How do healing agents take care of themselves? Dr. Malone reasons that healing agents and the people they are trying to heal are two sides of the same coin. That is, one's well-being is dependent on the relationship of people and things to which one is connected.[2]

Listed below are additional concepts and practices recommended by health professionals for healthcare providers (that I feel are relevant for ministry leaders, too, since we provide a form of health care) that one can adapt and practice for better self-care.[3]

- **Avoid the stormy personality.** Try your best not to create chaos. Know what you can control and what you can avoid.
- **Know yourself/self-reflection.** Knowing yourself, your idiosyncrasies, and what you enjoy and dislike should influence how you spend your time.
- **Manage your anxiety.** You may be anxious about something, but you must know how to address it. You can do so by choosing to slow down and pace yourself as you work and breathe.
- **Have a workspace.** For those who work from home, create a workspace, and only do work at that

space. Make sure you take breaks and downtime by stepping away from the space. This can help combat the feelings of being overwhelmed and anxious.

- **Be Flexible.** Exhibit the essential flexibility of a tree. That is, stay grounded and rooted in your core beliefs and faith, but find time to move with the shifting winds of crisis without being uprooted. Allow your faith and connection with God to sustain you.

The pandemic afforded me the opportunity to look more closely at the practice of self-care. In some ways, I practiced it, but a careful assessment of my life revealed that I was neglecting it, too. Listed below are some self-care methods that have proven to keep me secure and confident amidst the COVID-19 pandemic.

Spiritual Self-Care

In a previous chapter, we spoke about the importance of devotion. Prayer, meditation on Scripture, and being still before the Lord are all forms of self-care. Time spent in the presence of God is priceless. In these intimate moments, our God provides the spiritual care that encourages and energizes us to continue our service unto God. There is no replacement for this kind of spiritual self-care.

Scripture reminds us that if we draw nigh to God, God will draw nigh unto us (James 4:8). There is a reason why Jesus ventured away in the morning to pray. Sitting quietly with God is therapeutic as the Holy Spirit reminds us of who God is and how we fit into His plan for the church.

Ministry can be taxing spiritually. It is a complicated milieu of demands, emotions, people, and unrealistic expectations. It is important to set boundaries and protect the precious commodity of time. This includes time for you and time with God. As you pour out unto God in service, allow God to pour into you during your time of devotion. Allow God to restore your soul.

The word *restore* as David uses it in Psalm 23:3 means "to return or turn back." It is to bring back to an original state or grant restitution for what has been lost. In intimate moments with God, the Lord will restore to you the pieces of you that you have emptied. Akin to a restoration project of a home where the original wood floors are discovered and refurbished, the Lord can repair you.

The wear and tear of ministry can feel as if people, policies, predicament, and procedures have walked and trampled on your soul; but one word from the Holy Spirit in a still, small voice can liberate and empower you to thrive. It will make you feel brand-new because it has come from the God who makes all things new (Revelation 21:4-5). Pastor and leader, spend time with God for you and your health. Allow Jesus Christ by the power of the Holy Spirit to breathe on you (John 20:22).

Physical Self Care

Much has been written about the importance of physical health. We live in an age when people are becoming more health conscious about food and lifestyle choices. The taxation of ministry calls for pastors and leaders to be in good health. Exercise and proper dieting are the vital elements of self-care. This has become more apparent in the pandemic.

Many of my colleagues have joined the Peleton movement and have virtual home gyms. During the pandemic, our ministry provided virtual exercise and cooking classes to help encourage a healthy lifestyle. It is important to have some form of movement during the day. You can decide how much time and what regiment works for you. Please consult with your physician to see the best plan of health. Too many leaders are succumbing to illness that results from a lack of exercise and a poor diet. Perhaps one area that can help improve our health is proper rest.

In COVID worship, I was reintroduced into the importance of rest. The accelerated pace of ministry forced me to take time to rest if I desired to be an effective leader. Because of the shift in our ministry approaches and methods for virtual worship, I had to rely more on the gifting of my staff and team. Ministering in a pandemic opened my mind and eyes to more of God's possibilities. I discerned that it is okay to take periods of rest and that in doing so I was not being lazy or apathetic. I was following God.

Our bodies need rest. We are not perpetual machines without the need to stop. It is crucial that we take time to power off. Sleep is the activity that helps our bodies recalibrate. To be effective at anything, we must have an adequate amount of sleep. Much has been said and written about physical health, but one area of health has been neglected in my context and culture in ministry: Mental health is a critical area of self-care that has been undervalued, if not overlooked.

Mental Self-Care

The importance of mental health in the pandemic has been elevated. The sharp and swift changes in our normative modes of living in the COVID world have compromised our mental health. The mental health of essential workers, especially our medical professionals, have suffered drastically in the pandemic. It is understandable.

Hospital custodians and cafeteria workers, sanitation workers, restaurant employees, grocery store employees, first-responders, public transportation employees, and people who could not afford to stay home were afraid, nervous, anxious, or all of the above.

Many of these brave individuals have developed cases of anxiety because it is the body's natural response to stress. They have suffered from feelings of being overwhelmed, apprehensive, worried, distressed, and fearful because of the lack of resources and necessary equipment.

The pandemic has created an atmosphere for anxiety and depression to flourish, and it worsens when a stressful event approaches.[4] The number of COVID-19 cases continued to increase alongside mounting fatalities. The pandemic has been the culprit to the alarming number of those unemployed.

According to a Census Bureau Survey, in the spring of 2020, one in three Americans reported symptoms of depression or anxiety, more than three times the rate from a similar survey conducted in the first half of 2019. And due to social distancing, people go long periods without seeing family and friends, which can be deeply harmful to one's mental state.

Anxiety, as a form of fear, forged an atmosphere in COVID.[5] Mental health professionals have concluded that the pandemic created a mental health crisis. Dr. Paul Duberstein, public health psychologist and professor at the Rutgers School of Public Health, says, "Families spending more time with each other in confined spaces will have unintended consequences, such as increased rates of battering, domestic violence and murder-suicide."[6] The coronavirus pandemic has been counterproductive to maintaining a healthy state of mind, and no one seems to be exempt.

In her podcast on Spotify, Michelle Obama, former first lady of the United States, revealed that she was suffering from low-grade depression during the pandemic.

Obama said the culprits to her mental state were the pandemic, race relations in the United States, and the political strife of it all. In an article, she wrote, "I'm waking up in the middle of the night because I'm worrying about something or there's a heaviness. . . . I try to make sure I get a workout in, although there have been periods throughout this quarantine, where I just have felt too low."[7]

In a *USA Today* article concerning the mental health impact of the coronavirus, Dr. Katheryn Smerling wrote, "Too many people suffer because they don't make their needs known."[8] It is wise to seek help through a licensed medical professional, a therapist, or a psychologist. Talk medicine known as therapy is invaluable. It is what we do informally or formally with our friends, pastors, and counselors.

In 2019, our ministry created Shiloh C.A.R.E.S. (Counseling to Aide in Restoring and Encouraging Souls). We have trained biblical counselors who provide a safe space for talk therapy. It is an introduction into therapy and counseling. It is not meant to be a licensed practice. Therefore, we are in partnership with other licensed professional therapists, clinicians, and practices if ongoing therapy is needed for more advanced challenges.

This ministry has been a blessing to our community. Interestingly, most if not all of those who have relied on this service are members of the community and not our church. God's prompting and leading to form this ministry has helped others. But in this pandemic, I did not realize how I was neglecting my own mental health, so I sought help.

In May 2020, I met with a therapist. I chose the organization Safe Harbor, a Christian counseling service. Talk medicine proved to be invaluable to me. Although I have not suffered from anxiety or depression, my therapist helped me grasp alternative understandings of how it can adversely affect people. My therapist encouraged me to think differently.

The counselor confronted me on the ways I function and operate, challenged my understanding of myself, and exposed inconsistencies in my approach to marriage and ministry. My therapist worked from a strength-based counseling approach and perspective that proved to be invaluable for my development as a leader and improvement as a husband. After every session, I felt convicted yet empowered to serve and lead better.

I cannot underscore enough the importance of mental health for pastors. You must create the space and take the initiative to sit down and talk with a professional counselor or coach. You give so much of yourself as you entertain the emotions and perspectives of others.

You need a place to speak, if not vent, your frustrations so that you do not spew your irritations on your staff and family. One outburst and lack of self-control can do extensive damage to the emotional health of those around you.

What is more, it will cause the people you lead to question your integrity.

Even if you feel that you can handle and have handled pastoring in a crisis well, it is still okay to see a therapist. Talk medicine will offer you an alternative to enhance your leadership skills and improve your mental health. I believe that the Holy Spirit can speak through licensed and trained individuals who have a desire to see people like you be well. Perhaps the best use of talk therapy is regarding an area that the church is all too familiar with: the response to the unavoidable reality of death.

The pandemic presented enough reasons to place emphasis on mental health in the area of grief. Our counseling ministry saw the most traffic and inquiries regarding grief. The pandemic has contributed greatly to this truth. Grief related to death is the portion of the human experience that is inexplicable. Who knows the correct and proper way to deal with death? Because of the coronavirus, many churches have had to alter the means through which we offer support for grieving families.

With all the turmoil, tragedy, and terror among us due to the COVID-19 virus, the one place that would normally be filled during times like these is the house of God. In a crisis, it was customary for the people of God to flood to the tabernacle. Our faith tradition and Scripture suggest that in crises or times of trouble, we journey to the temple to meet with God.

But in the pandemic, the word of the psalmist becomes inappropriate. We could no longer say, "I was glad when they said unto me, let us go into the house of the LORD" (Psalm 122:1, KJV). We could not "enter into his gates with thanksgiving, and into his courts with praise" (Psalm 100:4, KJV). No one was able to "go into His tabernacle" and "worship at His footstool" (Psalm 132:7, NKJV).

Additionally, we could not hold life celebrations in the sanctuary. We were unable to sing the songs of the tradition and faith in community. In my context, the process of healing the heart begins at the homegoing service and the repast. There is a longstanding custom of fellowship at the table with food to comfort and liberate the soul. This time of sharing in community with food is a critical portion of the overall ecclesiology.

The testimonial sharing at the repast helps promote an ecclesiology that yields a "liberating wisdom that moves persons toward liberation and hope-building vocation."[8] The hope is that in these moments, God begins to heal wounded souls and broken hearts. This is a crucial and sacred act of church in my context.

But virtual pastoral care can feel distant and inauthentic. For the pastors whose members of the congregation and family who were transitioning weekly, the pressure of performing while grieving was immense. The coronavirus placed death at the forefront of our reality.

I have spoken with many colleagues in ministry who informed me that they were connected in some form or fashion to multiple people who have succumbed to the grip of COVID-19. The pain and uncertainty of our time can be unbearable. Perhaps, this is when speaking with a trained therapist is vital to the mental health of religious professionals.

A therapist can help you process and repurpose your thoughts and emotions. Frankly, it is good to talk through your emotions and uncover the root of your distress. Grieving is a life-long process, and therapy is an essential partner for the journey. Self-care has caused me to be an advocate and to be more vigilant of things that everyone can do to ensure that their mental health is intact. Regarding ministry, it has helped me repurpose my priorities in life. One of those urgencies is the importance of sabbath and family.

Importance of Sabbath

During the Day of Atonement festival, the practice of a sabbath (Leviticus 23:32) was required for the community. The sabbath is a day of solemn rest when no work is to be done. The sabbath, *shabbat* in Hebrew, is the seventh day of the week, designated as the day of rest for God, who rested in the Creation story of Genesis.[9] Yahweh commanded Moses and Israel to observe this day as one of the commandments (Exodus 20:8-11).

The sabbath is not the Lord's Day, Sunday, the day we as Christians worship in commemoration of the resurrection of Jesus Christ. There is no Christian sabbath. However, I do believe that the biblical concept of sabbath can be applied to pastors and leaders. There should be one day that the pastor protects and preserves for rest. In this light, a personal sabbath is in itself a form of self-care.

A number of mentors encouraged me to keep a "figurative" sabbath day in the week of my choosing. It was to be a form of rejuvenation and renewal through rest. This day would be when I chose not to work but relax. It is practical if leaders can afford such liberty as part of their lifestyle. I am aware that many bi-vocational leaders are unable to claim a sabbath. For those who can, the model of a day of rest is beneficial for clarity and self-care.

I became more aware of my need for a sabbath during the quarantine church. Because of the new normal, ministry was moving at such a fast pace. The additional meetings with ministry teams and ministry partners, coupled with the communication changes and troubleshooting of our systems took a toll.

My wife mentioned that my work life seemed to speed up for me. At home, the children were beginning to think that my laptop was synonymous with work. My children would constantly ask when I would be finished with work so I could be available to them.

At first, I was opposed to the idea of sabbath in crisis because the times were too critical. But I soon remembered my own theology regarding ministry. The church belongs to God. This church where I serve as pastor existed before I did. I am not the driving force of its existence, but the Holy Spirit is. If God rested and required that His congregation do so in antiquity, then surely I could observe some form of it for my mental health.

In my sabbath time, I realized that every problem is not a crisis and every member's issue is not my crisis. As a pastor, I cannot fall victim to invoking the savior syndrome where I become the answer to every difficulty that is presented. Having a sabbath kept, and continues to keep, my ego in check.

Also, during my weekly sabbath, the Lord reminded me that I am to continually direct people to Him. My intervention into the lives of His church at every moment could hinder the growth and sanctification process of His children. Simply stated, there are some people issues of which I am to avoid because God desires to do a transformative work in His people. Afterall, it is God's church!

As I continue to seek God and lean not to my own understanding but acknowledge Him, the Lord promises to give direction (Proverbs 3:5-6). More important, I have no desire to put my family at risk of losing their husband and father. The initial period of quarantine helped me to further see the value of family prioritization.

Family Matters

Before the creation of the church, there was the family; however, the people who are often neglected in ministry are members of the family unit. I have heard multiple stories from colleagues and have received more wisdom from my elders that the family must be first in ministry.

Unfortunately, too many of my colleagues in ministry are divorced or have unhealthy marriages. When I inquired about what went wrong, they immediately told me that they failed to place the needs of their spouses before the church. They made concessions for their children, but their spouses often resented the church due to the demands of ministry. They did not set clear boundaries regarding their family and the ministry. They made a clear choice to prioritize the ministry over their marriage.

As a pastor who is married, I understand how ministry can be perceived as the other obligation in the family unit, but the truth is that it has no such place in the marriage. The church is the bride of Christ. When pastors uphold the church before their families, they are proverbially committing adultery. The church belongs to God! Christ should be our first love and not His church.

Most of us know that Christ and the church are not identical. God is bigger than His church. God is perfect and His church, filled with imperfect people, is flawed. It is important for pastors and leaders to establish clear boundaries to protect their time and their families. Fortunately, I learned this early in my marriage. This theological position is what accentuated my relationship with my wife.

My wife is the daughter of a pastor. She is a preacher's kid, or PK. She told the Lord that she had no desire to marry a pastor or a minister. When we were dating, she informed me on numerous occasions that in her childhood she longed to spend time with her parents, especially on Sundays. Rarely, did her father make it home in time for dinner on Sundays because his entire life revolved around the church. As a child, she felt that the church deprived her of moments with her father. She saw the damage that ministry can do to a family when leaders do not handle it properly.

My father-in-law is no longer a pastor because of his health. Since pastoring, he has had multiple heart attacks and strokes. The stresses of ministry took a toll on his mental and physical being. The pressures of trying to be all things to all people was simply too much.

Given the sentiments of my wife and her outlook on marriage and ministry, I made a promise to her never to place the ministry before her. My wife and I have had intense conversations about who I need to be for the church and that what happened to her father would not happen to me. I came into our relationship promising that she would be the priority after God, followed by our children and then the church. This dynamic was tested early in our courtship.

One evening while we were out enjoying our first official date as a couple, I received a phone call from a member saying her young adult child had died unexpectedly. My first inclination was to tell my wife (who was my girlfriend at the time) that I had an unexpected emergency and had to leave. As I was on my way to do that, I was reminded of the promise I made to her. I phoned another minister from the church to reach out to the member, who then received an outpouring of pastoral care from other ministers and church members.

The next morning, I reached out to the mother and prayed with her and eventually made a visit to her home. To see if I had made the proper decision at that moment, I spoke with one of my trusted ministry colleagues who was married. He ensured me that I was correct to prioritize and protect my time. The beauty of pastoral care is that the church can administer it as part of the priesthood of believers (1 Peter 2:5). This advice would prove to be invaluable for my self-care and the primacy of placing my wife and family first.

As I began to candidate for the position of senior pastor, our stance on marriage and ministry would be questioned again. In fact, when I was interviewing for the position at the ministry where I currently serve, the search committee asked to meet with me and my wife. The team posed a question to my wife about her expectations of ministry. She responded emphatically by conveying to them her family history. She explained that she was a daughter of a pastor who experienced firsthand the dangers of ministry life. She then made a bold request in the interview.

She told the search committee that Sundays were for worship and then family. That is, after Sunday worship, it is family time. She does not subscribe to church programs on Sunday or having unnecessary meetings on the Lord's Day. I heard my wife speak clearly and so did the search committee.

When I was elected pastor, they assured me that they would honor my wife's desire because they could hear the sincerity and seriousness in her voice. Moreover, my predecessor retired because of health reasons. He became ill, and his physicians declared that he was unable to physically fulfill the duties of senior pastor. I heard and continue to hear from God through my gift, my wife.

To preserve our boundaries, I instituted a policy that no church business or meetings were to be held on Sunday when I became senior pastor. Sunday is the Lord's Day when we worship, but Sunday seemed like a workday for me. I arrived at church by 7:00 AM and would not leave the campus until 1:30 or 2:00 PM. We held two services at 8:00 AM and 11:00 AM.

Sundays were taxing and draining, but time with my family on Sunday after worship energized me. It provided an opportunity to see the value of family and what is my priority. The quarantine church during COVID presented new opportunities to help enhance, if not redefine, the importance of family.

At the outset of the pandemic, we changed the time of our worship service. The most convenient time for worship is 10:00 AM. Our virtual worship service is usually no longer than 75 minutes each Sunday. At the most, I would spend three hours at church since I preach and stream live from the sanctuary. Customarily, I leave at 9:00 AM and return by noon. Other times when we prerecord a service or replay a former service, I have the luxury of remaining home.

Now, Sunday has become more of a family day. My wife has expressed her appreciation for her family on Sundays and the executive decisions that I have made regarding Sunday worship. In this quarantine period, my wife has discovered a new passion for meal preparation and presentation. I come home to a delicious and delightful brunch that I now eat with my family. It is a joy to come home to freshly prepared French toast, pastries, and an assortment of breads, bacon, and eggs. Brunch has become family time.

In this new space, I am not as fatigued as I once was. My wife has expressed the relief she feels for Sundays because she no longer has to prepare church outfits and get toddlers ready to come to the sanctuary. My children seem happier and are excited to see me return on Sundays. It has been a refreshing time for my family.

In this moment, I firmly believe that God is resetting priorities for ministry. He is placing the family in the foreground and calling for husbands and wives to consider ministry to be family-first oriented.

My wife and I feel stronger and closer as a result of the quarantine ministry. We have discussed our differences and voiced the areas where we feel growth is necessary in our union. The intimate time we share as a family on Sundays has improved my mental health and given an additional contribution to my self-care. Family matters.

Pastors and leaders, I implore you to prioritize your family. The church can and will survive without you. Please do your best to train up leaders so that you feel you do not have to do everything. The ministry should be able to run efficiently, even when you are absent. This will be a testimony to the culture you create and the systems you implement. Know how your spouse fits into your ministry, and include your spouse in the decisions you make. This has proven to be valuable for me.

There is no executive decision of which I do not have my wife's perspective. When I seek God for the "what" and "why," God often speaks through my wife regarding the "how." Every decision you make as pastor will have an effect on your spouse and family. It could be a positive life-changing one or a negative tension-creating one that will damage your integrity and their trust in you. Please know where your spouse fits into the ministry. Take the time to encourage your spouse to seek God to discern how His purpose for him or her will flourish in ministry.

The ministry where you serve will never be about you. You are an important piece to the ministry as you honor God. But remember, you are replaceable. Neither your ministry nor your marriage will flourish in a healthy capacity until your spouse and children know how they are part of the ministry. Their knowledge of this is your responsibility.

My experience as pastor has taught me this truth. Some of the most effective sermons that I have preached, according to my congregation and leadership, have been when I adamantly took care of the needs of my family. Often, ministry issues would arise, or my wife and children needed my attention at moments I ordinarily would use for sermon preparation or enhancing.

In those places, where I felt that I was not as thoroughly prepared as I should have been, God did wonders in the moment. I feel strongly that God blessed the word to His people and favored me in the moment due to the decision I made to place my family first.

Pastor, it is easier to find a new ministry or a pastorate than it is to repair the emotional scars and damage that spawns from neglect of family. You can lead another ministry more quickly than you can manufacture a healthy family unit. Please humble yourself, forego your ego, and prioritize your family. It is necessary for your self-care.

Leader Examination

- How important is self-care for you? What self-care practices have you implemented since the pandemic? Do you practice sabbath (rest)?

- Has your mental health suffered as a result of the pandemic? What are the stressors (inevitable, imposed, and chosen) that affect your peace and mental health?

- What boundaries have you constructed that are non-negotiables to preserve your mental health? If you have a family, how do you prioritize their well-being and their mental health?

- Are you an advocate of talk medicine (therapy)? Does your ministry advocate for mental health?

Prayer for Pandemic Pastors and Leaders:

God, I come to You in the name of Jesus. I relinquish all that I am to receive all that You call me to be. Lord, help me to understand that the best self I can offer You is all of me.

I hear Your word by Your Spirit: "Come to me, all you who are weary and burdened, and I will give you rest. Take my yoke upon you and learn from me, for I am gentle and humble in heart, and you will find rest for your souls. For my yoke is easy and my burden is light" (Matthew 11:28-30, NIV).

Ministry is a heavy burden, and I come to You for strength, healing, and hope. Renew my mind, and remind me that I find safety in You. Reveal to me the places where I need to improve my physical, spiritual, and mental health. Reveal to me professional men and women who are lovers of You to help me maintain my sanity in this burdensome joy. I carve out time to rest securely in You. Help me to care for my family as You care for Your church. I can rest in You because You are the God who does not slumber nor sleep.

Since You are watching over Your church, restore my soul that I can serve You and Your people in confidence. In the moments when I am doubtful, help recall to me the truth that the joy of the Lord is my strength. I love You, Lord. I ask this prayer in the name of Jesus. Amen.

---

[1]Beverly Malone, PhD, RN, FAAN, CEO of National League of Nursing. Interview by author, Alexandria, Virginia, April 15, 2021.

[2]Ibid.

[3]H. L. Coons, S. Berkowitz, and R. A. David, "Self-Care Advice for Health-Care Providers During Covid-19," American Psychological Association Services, Inc. (March, 2020) https://www.apaservices.org/practice/ce/self-care/health-providers-covid-19.

[4]Kimberly Holland, https://www.healthline.com/health/anxiety.

[5]Paul Duberstein, "The Mental Health Fallout From COVID-19 Will Be Huge" (April 24, 2020) www.nj.com.

[6]"Michelle Obama Says She's Suffering From 'Low-Grade Depression,'" Allison Gordon, Thursday, August 6, 2020, CNN.com.

[7]"Find Things That Anchor You: Virtual Therapy, Other Ways to Get Social Support Amid Coronavirus," Hannah Yasharoff, *USA Today* (April 23, 2020).

[8]Ann E. Streaty Wimberly, *Soul Stories: African American Christian Education* (Nashville: Abingdon Press, 1994), 33.

[9]M. S. Heiser, "The Sabbath," *Faithlife Study Bible* (Bellingham, WA: Lexham Press, 2012, 2016).

CHAPTER SEVEN

DISCERNING THE TIMES FOR PROPHETIC UTTERANCE

"Now as He sat on the Mount of Olives, the disciples came to Him privately, saying, 'Tell us, when will these things be? And what will be the sign of Your coming, and of the end of the age?' And Jesus answered and said to them: 'Take heed that no one deceives you. For many will come in My name, saying, "I am the Christ," and will deceive many. And you will hear of wars and rumors of wars. See that you are not troubled; for all these things must come to pass, but the end is not yet. For nation will rise against nation, and kingdom against kingdom. And there will be famines, pestilences, and earthquakes in various places. All these are the beginning of sorrows.'" (Matthew 24:3-8, NKJV)

I N my time of prayer and consultation, the Holy Spirit led me to this text in Matthew. I wrestled with the text, hoping to give a word from the Lord. In my estimation, it was clear as to what was happening in the world. An unseen and inexplicable event had infiltrated our norms and shifted our way of life.

When the entire world was on lockdown, the Lord our God had to be speaking to His church. This is my attempt to convey what the Spirit was saying to Shiloh and to the church during this time. This is the prophetic utterance to the body of Christ in my context. It is not to serve as prophecy or as a word of warning, but more so a prophetic affirmation of the words of Jesus Christ in the gospel concerning His return. The pandemic is a pestilence that has claimed the lives of many in our world. I pray that we as the church will prepare continually for Christ's return by humbly subjecting ourselves to a righteous and holy life before our Lord.

This sermon was preached for our first service in COVID worship, Sunday, March 22, 2020. It was our 157th church anniversary at Shiloh Baptist Church in Alexandria, Virginia:

There is no escaping the reality that we are in a new normal. Professionals who work remotely are now commonplace. Rush-hour traffic needs a new name because no one is in a rush. Social distancing (six feet apart) is now the appropriate form of fellowship. Grocery stores are filled with people, but they lack toilet tissue, paper towels, napkins, ground beef, Clorox wipes, and Lysol. Movie theatres, theme parks, and restaurants are vacant; but take-out, pick-up, and drive-thru are bustling, and GrubHub is doing well.

Our schools are vacant. Parents are now provider and professor with lesson plans, hoping to maintain some sense of routine learning for their children. Maybe now, our country and communities will have a greater appreciation for teachers and educators.

With all the turmoil, tragedy, and terror among us due to the COVID-19 virus, the one place that would normally be filled during times like these is the house of God. In a crisis, people flood to the tabernacle. It is what the Scriptures and traditions of our faith suggest.

We are called to journey and celebrate coming to the temple to meet with God, for the word says, "I was glad when they said unto me, let us go into the house of our LORD." "Enter into his gates with thanksgiving and into his court with praise." "Let us go into his tabernacle; Let us worship at his footstool." "Praise the LORD! Praise God in his Sanctuary!" "For a day in thy courts is better than a thousand; I would rather be a doorkeeper in the house of my God, than to dwell in the tents of wickedness."

But given the pandemic of the coronavirus, even houses of worship are empty. There are no parking lot attendants, no greeters or ushers, no choirs in robes, no marching to give an offering or passing of the plate, no altars filled with those who have requests to lay before God, no diaconate or ministerial team to welcome people to Christ. In trying times like these, it is customary to be in the house of

God. But as people of the Book who respect the laws of our land, even houses of worship are vacant.

People need the Lord but cannot come to the house of the Lord because it may be detrimental to their health. This begs the question, Where can we go to worship God if you are not the pastor, audiovisual technician, streaming consultant, band member, or praise team leader?

Times like these call us to question our worship practices and theology, yet this same Scripture that calls us to question our praxis is simultaneously the same word that strengthens and encourages us to worship our God. No matter what our reality, the truth remains. The word of God through the prophet Isaiah was correct: "The grass withers, the flowers fade, but our God shall stand forevermore" (Isaiah 40:8, KJV).

The brick and mortar of the worship space or house of God does not compromise or confuse the character of our God. No matter where we are, our God is still worthy to be praised! No matter the happenings of our world, our God is still worthy to be praised! Whether I am in my house at the kitchen table, on the sofa with my family and not fully dressed, in the man cave with surround sound, or in the bathroom with a cellphone in my hand to stream the service, the name of the Lord our God is worthy to be praised! And here is my reason: No matter where I am, God is!

The Spirit of the Lord our God is not relegated to the walls of 1401 Jamieson Avenue or 1401 Duke Street or

1429 Duke Street in Alexandria, Virginia 22314—or any physical location. No matter where you are, God is. God is still omnipotent (all-powerful), God is still omniscient (all-knowing), and God is still omnipresent (everywhere). There is nowhere we can venture, traverse, or journey where God is not.

David said, "Where can I go from Your Spirit? Or where can I flee from Your presence? If I ascend into heaven, You are there; If I make my bed in hell, behold, You are there. If I take the wings of the morning, And dwell in the uttermost parts of the sea, Even there Your hand shall lead me, And Your right hand shall hold me" (Psalm 139:7-10, NKJV).

This is the word of the Lord this morning: Wherever you are, God is! Shiloh, whether you are at home, in your car on the way to the supermarket, or in the sanctuary, God is!

- God is still the Ancient of Days!

- God is still the Alpha and Omega!

- God is still the All-Sufficient God. Even in a crisis, God is!

- And from everlasting to everlasting, He is still God!

So, wherever you are, can you help me give this God some glory? "This is the day that the LORD has made and we shall rejoice and be glad in it!" (Psalm 118:24, NKJV).

Wherever you are, can you help me give this God some glory? For "the earth is the LORD's and the fullness thereof" (Psalm 24:1, NKJV).

Wherever you are, can you help me give this God some glory? For He is still "the King of Glory, The LORD God strong and mighty, mighty in battle!" (Psalm 24:8, NKJV).

You and I should have a made-up mind that in the midst of the coronavirus pandemic, we will be the church of the living God! Whether we gather virtually through computers, cellphones, tablets, or stream through the television, we need to make a vow to "bless the LORD at all times, his praises shall continually be in my mouth" (Psalm 34:1, NKJV). That even as I worship my God, I woke up this morning! So, I make a choice to "be thankful unto Him and bless His name!" (Psalm 100:4, NKJV).

In the midst of this pandemic, I wonder is there anybody out there who still has the Holy Ghost resolve to declare and proclaim by faith that "the LORD is good, his mercy is everlasting and his truth endures throughout all generations!" (Psalm 100:5, NKJV). Is there anybody out there who knows that if I can't gather with saints in the sanctuary, I still choose to bless the name of the Lord?

Yet some may raise the relevant question, How can we bless the Lord in such times as these? How can we bless the name of our God when there are over 304,000 confirmed cases in the world due to the coronavirus? How can we bless the name of our God when the death toll has reached close to 13,000 in the world due to the coronavirus? How can we bless the name of our God when the death toll has excceeded 4,000 in Italy alone, surpassing the 3,400 people in China? How can we bless the name of our God when the world cannot even get a handle on this unseen virus?

We bless the Lord because we as the kingdom of God know that we are inching closer to the return of Christ. Our Lord said that He was coming back! And in these times, we are witnessing the beginning of sorrows! America, world, and church, Jesus is coming back!

In our text this morning, Jesus describes our current existential reality. Some 2,000 years ago, He said things akin to the COVID-19 would occur as a precursor to His return. Church, we are living in the last days. He says this clearly in our text.

Verses 6-8 say, "And you will hear of wars and rumors of wars. See that you are not troubled; for all these things must come to pass, but the end is not yet. For nation will rise against nation, and kingdom against kingdom. And there will be famines, pestilences, and earthquakes in various places. All these are the beginning of sorrows."

Our entire world is in panic mode as we grapple with this pandemic. Life as we know it will not be the same.

School systems may be reoriented. Certainly, our health-care system needs to be addressed because this pandemic has exposed lies and inconsistences in how health needs are handled.

Economic disparity is more on display. How is it that the government has money to hand out now as if it was not necessary to the downtrodden and poor before? This country could operate with economic justice if it so desired because you find the finances for what you desire to finance. So maybe the morality of our nation or the lack of it is now front and center to the world. He's coming back!

But we the people of God carry a different hope! Our ultimate hope is not in the executive, legislative, or judicial branches of these United States! Our hope is rooted and remains in our Lord Jesus Christ. We recognize that God desires that we accelerate our mode of preparation for His return.

These times are akin to preparing for a big meal. I love that it is getting warmer. I am reminded of how my father and mother would prepare for the family barbecue during the Fourth of July: pork shoulders, Boston butt, ribs, chicken, pork chops, hamburgers, potato salad, garden salad, corn on the cob, peach cobbler, and freshly made sun tea that bakes outside in the sun with fresh mint leaves from the side of the house.

All the food is prepared the day of, but there is major preparation beforehand. Before you cook, you must season the meat and gather all the ingredients. The purchasing of ingredients to make the meal happens before the meal is prepared. There is preparation before the feast!

In our text, Jesus is preparing the disciples for His pending crucifixion where He would purchase our salvation. Jesus instructed them about the things to come that we are currently witnessing. And now since we have been purchased, Jesus our Lord is preparing us for a meal called the Last Supper. This is when we the church, who is the bride of Christ, will sit down and feast in eternity. Jesus Christ is coming back!

2020 is a pivotal year in the preparation for His return. So, I pray that your vision becomes clearer as we learn how to prepare for the return of Christ. One of the prerequisites in our preparation is to do what the disciples did in our text. We need to make it a habit to meet Jesus in the Mount of Olives. You must discover your Mount of Olives.

Verse 3 says, "Now as He sat on the Mount of Olives, the disciples came to Him privately, saying, 'Tell us, when will these things be? And what will be the sign of Your coming, and of the end of the age?'"

The Mount of Olives is a small ridge of three summits, about two miles long, the highest of which is not quite 3,000 feet above sea level. It runs north to south across from the Kidron Valley, east of Jerusalem, and is known for its abundance of olive trees.[1] The main range of mountains runs through the central and southern portions of Palestine from the north to the south.[2] The Mount of Olives is where David fled from Jerusalem after his son Absalom led a successful revolt and took the path that led over the crest of the Mount of Olives as he made his way to his temporary exile in the Transjordan (2 Samuel 15:30).[3]

Jesus' destination on the Mount of Olives was the garden of Gethsemane (Matthew 26:36). It is here during the evenings of the Passion Week, Jesus tarried (Luke 21:37). It is here Jesus agonized before His Father in prayer (Matthew 26:30, 36ff; Mark 14:26, 32ff; Luke 22:30ff; John 18:1ff).[4]

They met with Jesus privately in Jesus' prayer closet. During this troublesome and trying time in Jesus' life, our Lord and Savior communed with the Father. Jesus received comfort, strength, and endurance for the dangerous destiny of the Crucifixion. It was on the Mount of Olives where Jesus' prayers intensified and sweat like drops of blood cascaded down His face! It was on the Mount of Olives where the angel from heaven strengthened Him for the ensuing torture of Calvary!

The Mount of Olives in the garden of Gethsemane was the place of prayer and preparation to do the will of God. During this time, prayer and communion with God is vital! Every believer needs a Mount of Olives, a place where you can meet with God in private. It is there where your confidence in God is strengthened! It is there where you hear God whisper words of power for your endurance! It is there where you meet with God to find peace in the midst of your chaos! It is there where your vision becomes clear! It is there where you maintain your sanity as God encourages you that you are not alone! It is there where you can hear one word from the Lord that will comfort your soul, convict you of your life, and corral you to return to your first love that is Christ.

Yes, the people of God should be sympathetic to and pray for those who suffer from the coronavirus. We must be shrewd during this time to maintain social distancing to prevent the spread of the virus in these suspicious times. However, the people of God should not be shook regarding COVID-19. We are sensitive to the times but not shaken by them, especially when you have been with God in the secret place (your Mount of Olives). This place is the living presence of God that goes with me even as I dwell in it.

You are not shaken by the calamities of the world—even as you grieve—when you meet with God, or rather when God meets you on your Mount of Olives. On the Mount of Olives, God speaks. It is where your faith is renewed! It is where you hear God and recall the hymns of the faith that express a theology of sovereignty, providence, and deliverance. Even in the midst of COVID-19, God can remind you, and you recall the songs of Zion!

When peace like a river, attendeth my way,
When sorrows like sea billows roll
Whatever my lot, thou hast taught me to say
It is well, it is well, with my soul
Though Satan should buffet, though trials should come,
Let this blest assurance control,
That Christ has regarded my helpless estate,
And hath shed His own blood for my soul
My sin, oh, the bliss of this glorious thought
My sin, not in part but the whole,
Is nailed to the cross, and I bear it no more,
Praise the Lord, praise the Lord, O my soul
It is well (it is well)
With my soul (with my soul)
It is well, it is well with my soul.[5]

For some of you, this may sound like a foreign language: It is well. And you ask, How can it be well? How can you say it is well? Because He is coming back! Why is it well? Because He is coming back! How do you know all is well? Because He is coming back! We are in the beginning of sorrows, and Christ is coming back!

For those of you who may not be from a traditional church, you are more of the R&B version, Al Green said it like this in 1986, "I know that everything is gonna be all right. He's coming back, like He said He would!"[6]

So where is your Mount of Olives? Where is the place that you meet with God? Where is your prayer closet?

Where is your place and when is your time of communion with God? The times are too critical for us not to seek the Lord. Can we not hear the Spirit of God calling us to return to Christ? Shiloh, friends, and guests, please discover your private Mount of Olives, and meet God! God is available!

It was in this place that Jesus taught the disciples about the end of the times and how to recognize the atmosphere for His coming. People spend time with God and God's word to stay in preparation, always ready to give an account for in whom and what you believe. For when you dwell in the secret place with God, you will not be deceived, nor will you be bound by trouble.

Listen to what Jesus tells His disciples in verses 4-8: "And Jesus answered and said to them: 'Take heed that no one deceives you. For many will come in My name, saying, "I am the Christ," and will deceive many. And you will hear of wars and rumors of wars. See that you are not troubled; for all these things must come to pass, but the end is not yet. For nation will rise against nation, and kingdom against kingdom. And there will be famines, pestilences, and earthquakes in various places. All these are the beginning of sorrows.' "

Christ is careful to employ words of wisdom that the times are deceptive. He desires that His disciples know exactly with whom they deal and what to expect. Certain things must come to pass. There are human and natural events in the world that are unavoidable. They must come to pass, but the word to the kingdom of God, to me and you is, Do not be troubled.

The word *troubled*, θροέω (*throeo*), means "to be frightened so as to cry aloud or make a clamour."[7] It means "to be alarmed and disturbed with terror." I do not mean to minimize the severity of our current situation. This virus is real! We must be wise in how we approach this pandemic. We should show concern for the world and our immediate community. Especially, the seasoned saints and elders of our church deserve special attention.

But the people of God should not be sounding the alarm in fear, terror, nor trepidation. The word of the Lord this morning is, Do not be troubled. The all-sufficient God whom we serve is fully aware of COVID-19. God knows about it, and God knows about you. God's only recommendation is that if you cry aloud for anything, you cry aloud unto Him, the Lord your God in worship!

It is time for "Father, I stretch my hand to thee." It is time for "It's me, it's me, it's me, O Lord, standing in the need of prayer." It is time for you to cry, "I need thee, O, I need thee!"

You can still make a joyful noise unto the Lord and shout unto God with a voice of triumph because you have a promise from God in the word! It is what David said: "For in the time of trouble He shall hide me in His pavilion; In the secret place of His tabernacle He shall hide me; He shall set me high upon a rock" (Psalm 27:5, NKJV).

This kind of pandemic may be new to us, but it is not unfamiliar to God. For our God, the one who knows the very numbers of hair on your head, says to you do not be troubled. For God has done too much for us unto this point for us to doubt God now. Just think about the terror that our ancestors lived under every day of their lives. The more I read the history of our nation, the more I discover how terrorizing life was for men, women, and children during those times. Why do you think enslaved Africans cried out to God?

- "Kum by Ya, My Lord (Come by Here)"

- "Wade in the Water"

- "Lord, Remember Me"

- "Oh, Mary Don't You Weep"

- "Oh, Brothers Don't Get Weary"

- "Didn't My Lord Deliver Daniel"

And the anthology of Negro spirituals that were birthed in the terrorism and pandemic of the Middle Passage, chattel slavery, slave codes, Reconstruction, and Jim and Jane Crow laws. If our ancestors, who saw trouble on every side, cried out to God so that we could be here some 157 years later, it makes sense that we should cry out to God! Is there anybody who can cry out to God in the midst of the coronavirus?

Is there anybody who can cry out to God in the midst of COVID-19? Is there anybody who can cry out to God in the midst of a pandemic? Is there anybody who can cry out to God to expedite the healing, or at least convince the powers that be to release the vaccine and give the medical professionals the help they need?

Just think about what has transpired in the last two decades!

- September 11, 2001, thousands were killed and set the USA at war with the Taliban.

- The war in Iraq in 2003-2006

- The killing of Saddam Hussein and Osama Bin Laden

- The wars in Afghanistan and Syria

- The ongoing wars between Israel and Palestine

- Civil unrest in Somalia, Rwanda, and Nigeria, where Christians are being murdered daily

And that is just to name a few. That does not include other conflicts among nations. But the word of our Lord this morning is, Do not be troubled! There is civil unrest in our own communities regarding the injustice of excessive force by law enforcement that lead to the death of unarmed African American men and women. We continue to fight the good fight for justice, but the word of our Lord is, Do not be troubled!

We have had earthquakes in the US and the world; earthquakes in China, Haiti, Chile, Italy, Mexico, Iran, and Puerto Rico. Natural disasters in the Dominican Republic, the Bahamas. Tsunamis in Indonesia and Japan. Fires in California. And amid all this calamity, Jesus says, "Do not be troubled!" Please remember the other pandemics that have claimed lives!

- The West Nile Virus of 2002

- The SARS Virus of 2003

- The Bird Flu of 2005

- The Ecoli Pandemic of 2006

- The H1N1 Swine Flu of 2009

- The Ebola Virus of 2014

- The Zika Vvirus of 2016

But the word of our Lord is the same to us as to His disciples: Do not be troubled! Perhaps the COVID-19 pandemic may be one of the world's deadliest of which we do not know its end. But the word of the Spirit to the kingdom of God is, Do not be troubled! We must remember that although we may not gather in the house of God at this moment, if we would venture to our Mount of Olives, we may discover the secret place of our God. And in the secret place of our God, we find peace in our trouble!

He who dwells in the secret place of the Most High, Shall abide under the shadow of the Almighty. I will say of the LORD, "He is my refuge and my fortress; My God, in Him I will trust." Surely He shall deliver you from the snare of the fowler and from the perilous pestilence. He shall cover you with His feathers, and under His wings you shall take refuge; his truth shall be your shield and buckler. You shall not be afraid of the terror by night, Nor of the arrow that flies by day, Nor of the pestilence that walks in darkness, nor of the destruction that lays waste at noonday. A thousand may fall at your side, and ten thousand at your right hand; But it shall not come near you. Only with your eyes shall you look, and see the reward of the wicked. Because you have made the LORD, who is my refuge, Even the Most High, your dwelling place, no evil shall befall you, nor shall any plague come near your dwelling; for He shall give His angels charge over you, to keep you in all your ways.

Child of God and people of the world, do not be troubled, but recognize that there is hope! There is hope because there is time. COVID-19 and other things must come to pass, but we have hope. The end is not yet. As we wait for Jesus to return, Jesus waits for me, you, and the world to come to Him. Church, that is the mercy of God!

Jesus says in verse 8 that we are just at the beginning of sorrow or birth pangs, but this is not the end. This means that there is time for all to come or return to Jesus. The Lord God is still the compassionate and gracious God who desires that you make your life count. Please prostrate yourself before God in repentance with thanksgiving, and discover the mercy of God!

Even in the midst of the pandemic, God shows mercy. It is the mercy of God to call you to Him or return to Him. God could have left you unto your own faculties, desires, destruction, and demise. But God who is still the Lord, "the compassionate and gracious God, slow to anger, abounding in love and faithfulness, maintaining love to thousands, and forgiving wickedness, rebellion and sin" (Exodus 34:6-7, NIV).

This God is saying, in this new normal with a serious pandemic that will cause many to suffer, it's not over! Your life is not over! The end is near, but it is not here! The arms of Christ are still open! The body of Christ, the church, is still open! The heart of God is still open! The gates of heaven are still open!

And God is still merciful! You have time to make a decision to enter into the family of faith and the team of salvation. We are closer to the end, but we are not yet at the end! Come to Jesus!

This is the mercy of the one who said, "Come to me, all you who are weary and burdened, and I will give you rest. Take my yoke upon you and learn from me, for I am gentle and humble in heart, and you will find rest for your souls. For my yoke is easy and my burden is light" (Matthew 11:28-30, NIV).

This is the mercy of the one who said, "I have come that they may have life, and that they may have it more abundantly" (John 10:10b, NKJV). This is the mercy of the one who said, "If I be lifted up I will draw all of humanity unto me." This is the drawing of Christ to His Creation. Christ wants you! That is mercy!

No one deserves this mercy of acceptance, especially given our actions, attitudes, and accidents toward God. But God in Christ Jesus stills says, "I want you!"

"God, who is rich in mercy, because of His great love with which He loved us" (Ephesians 2:4, NKJV). This God has not forgotten about us, and God is waiting. Give your life to Jesus so that you can rest in the security that when He comes, you go with Him. Because when you receive the salvation of God in Christ Jesus, you will receive your corona. Not the Corona with a lime on some beach, but a true corona!

COVID-19 is called the "coronavirus." *Corona* means "crown" in Spanish, and coronavirus is a category of viruses so named because of its appearance. It's covered with crown-like spikes. As of now, you would think the coronavirus is king because it is dominating the media cycles and has issued a deadly decree that has shifted existence as we know it. But please know that although this disease is serious, the coronavirus is not king, nor does it wear the crown.

But you and I who are the body of Christ, you do wear a corona. When you are saved, you have a corona on your way to the King who wears the corona as Lord of all. You have a helmet of salvation that is your crown of victory.[8]

And I pray that if the coronavirus seeks to visit you, it will see your helmet of salvation that is the crown of the Messiah on your head in the Spirit. That your helmet of salvation will be your protective covering dripped in the blood of the Jesus, that grants you access to the throne room of heaven. That you will be protected and healed until you see Jesus. Because Jesus is coming back! He's coming back!

- The true King who wears the corona is the beginning and the end.

- The true King who wears the corona is the bright and morning star.

- The true King who wears the corona is the faithful and true.

- The true King who wears the corona is my battle-ax and my help.

- The true King who wears the corona has been crowned King.

He's coming back!

- This is the one in whose hands my life is in.

- This is the one in whose hands your life is in.

- This is the one who shall determine the end because He is the beginning and the end.

- This is the one who has already defeated COVID-19 on a hill called Calvary.

Every disease in life—cancer, diabetes, AIDS/HIV, hypertension, lupus, ALS, whatever you have—has been defeated when Christ shed His blood! The Bible says, "But He was wounded for our transgressions, He was bruised for our iniquities; The chastisement for our peace was upon Him, And by His stripes we are healed" (Isaiah 53:5, NKJV). He died so that we may live, and no disease, death, hell, or the grave can keep Him down!

COVID-19 is real, but it is not eternal and everlasting! But my God is! Because the Bible says—Bless the name of the Lord!—"Early Sunday morning the King of kings and